D0968670

Selling to the
New Elite

DISCOVER THE SECRET TO WINNING
OVER YOUR WEALTHIEST PROSPECTS

Jim Taylor

Stephen Kraus

Doug Harrison

AMACOM

AMERICAN MANAGEMENT ASSOCIATION

New York • Atlanta • Brussels • Chicago • Mexico City • San Francisco
Shanghai • Tokyo • Toronto • Washington, D.C.

Bulk discounts available. For details visit: www.amacombooks.org/go/specialsales
Or contact special sales:
Phone: 800-250-5308 • E-mail: specialsls@amanet.org
View all the AMACOM titles at: www.amacombooks.org

This publication is designed to provide accurate and authoritative information in regard to the subject matter covered. It is sold with the understanding that the publisher is not engaged in rendering legal, accounting, or other professional service. If legal advice or other expert assistance is required, the services of a competent professional person should be sought.

Various names used by companies to distinguish their software and other products can be claimed as trademarks. A list of trademarked terms appearing in this book may be found on page vi. AMACOM uses such names throughout this book for editorial purposes only, with no intention of trademark violation. Individual companies should be contacted for complete information regarding trademarks and registration.

Library of Congress Cataloging-in-Publication Data
Taylor, Jim, 1947–
  Selling to the new elite : discover the secret to winning over your wealthiest prospects / Jim Taylor, Stephen Kraus, and Doug Harrison.
    p. cm.
  Includes index.
  ISBN-13: 978-0-8144-1653-2 (hardcover)
  ISBN-10: 0-8144-1653-5 (hardcover)
  1. Selling. 2. Affluent consumers. 3. Customer relations. I. Kraus, Stephen. II. Harrison, Doug, 1965– III. Title.
  HF5438.25.T387 2011
  658.85—dc22   2010039005

About AMA
American Management Association (www.amanet.org) is a world leader in talent development, advancing the skills of individuals to drive business success. Our mission is to support the goals of individuals and organizations through a complete range of products and services, including classroom and virtual seminars, webcasts, webinars, podcasts, conferences, corporate and government solutions, business books, and research. AMA's approach to improving performance combines experiential learning—learning through doing—with opportunities for ongoing professional growth at every step of one's career journey.

Printing number
10 9 8 7 6 5 4 3 2 1

To Ellie,
with *love*, *passion*, and *gratitude*
Jim

Trademarked Terms Appearing in *Selling to the New Elite*

Aeropostale

American Express

Apple

Armani

Baccarat

Beretta

BMW

Bulgari

Cartier

Chanel

Coach

Coca-Cola

Domaine de la
Romanée-Conti

Fendi

General Motors

Gucci

Hermès

IBM

Limoges

Louis Vuitton

Mercedes-Benz

Microsoft

Neiman Marcus

Prada

Radisson

Ritz Carlton

Rolex

Steuben

Tiffany

Timex

Vitamix

Volvo

Zales

Contents

CHAPTER ONE
The Desire to Acquire 5

Contents

Figures

Figures

Tables

Acknowledgments

We would like to thank the many people who contributed to this project with their time, energy, and forbearance . . .

- The staff at Harrison Group, including our Wealth Team of Don Winter, Kevin Sansone, Kevin Sturmer, and Emily Randolph

- The sales team at Harrison Group, including Burr Brown and Dan Merchant, who have tested and refined our techniques for sales success

- Our editorial team at AMACOM, particularly Christina Parisi and Erika Spelman

- Clients and colleagues who have given so much of themselves, particularly Carl Sewell of Sewell Motor Company, Jim Gold of Neiman Marcus, Bob Knebel of Flexjet, and Chip Besio of Southern Methodist University

We would particularly like to thank Cara David and the team at American Express Publishing, including Jackie Graziano, Kristy Bauer, and, of course, Ed Kelly. We appreciate all the work they have done with us and all that they enable us to do. We cannot thank you enough.

Most of all, we would like to thank the salespeople who graciously participated in our interviews and our training programs. They shared insights into their lives, their professions, and their passions—all with the hope of helping others achieve more fulfilling careers and lives.

SELLING TO THE NEW ELITE

Introduction

We have focused much of our work in the past five years on understanding wealthy individuals and luxury markets. We have worked with companies such as Mercedes-Benz, American Express, Cartier, Neiman Marcus, and many others. In other words, we have worked with companies for which luxury is not a preoccupation, but a passion. The same search for extraordinary quality also defines our clients who are not "luxury" providers, but are still exemplars of excellence in their categories—companies such as Microsoft, Coca-Cola, and Vitamix.

It is in passion, and with passion, that we find the greatest opportunity to sell.

We know how hard the last four years have been. Many have called it the Great Recession, with good reason, as it has already been far longer and more severe than any economic downturn since the Great Depression. Government economists tell us it began in December 2007, but our research identified spending cutbacks and an "emotional recession" as early as mid-2006. As of the writing of this book in September 2010, our research still suggests challenging times ahead for sales professionals. Despite the government's assertion that the recession ended in June 2009, over 90 percent of the affluent believe the recession still continues today, and over 60 percent expect it to continue for more than a year— attitudes that can easily become self-fulfilling prophecies. Most have reduced their spending. "I'll buy whatever I want" has been replaced with "Let's buy only what we need." The process has made them feel smart, not deprived, and most expect to continue their newfound frugality and value-orientation when and if the economy improves. The unfortunate bottom line: Today's economic challenges are unlikely to resolve themselves easily, deeply, or soon.

We know it has been hard to make your numbers.

Challenge, as always, creates opportunities. The desire to acquire runs deep in the human species, and despite their heightened value-orientation, the affluent continue to shop, particularly in categories they are passionate about.

Moreover, excellence is still valued. Despite the economy, the affluent have been reluctant to trade down—their expectations about and desires for quality, craftsmanship, and service have not diminished. Meanwhile, their expectations that purchases be thoughtful and meaningful have risen.

> **This is a book about how to sell,
> in these tough times, the very best things.**

We wrote this book primarily for those engaged in face-to-face selling of high-end products and services to financially successful individuals. But it is also of interest to those more tangentially related to that core mission, such as:

- Those who sell to the 90 percent who aren't affluent.

- Those who sell nonluxury products.

- Sales managers whose charge is to hire, grow, and retain top sales professionals.

- Advertising, marketing, and branding executives who try to build customer relationships "from afar"— through traditional and social media, through the products they create, through the brands they develop, through the retail experiences they design, through the corporate culture they build, and through the sales approach they instill directly and indirectly via hundreds of management decisions daily.

A WORD ABOUT OUR RESEARCH

Unless otherwise noted, data cited in this book are from our *Survey of Affluence and Wealth in America*, produced by Harrison Group and American Express Publishing. Now entering its fifth year, this industry-leading study of financially successful individuals is described more fully in the appendix. Throughout this book, for simplicity, we use the term "affluent" to describe the roughly 11 million U.S. households with at least $100,000 in annual discretionary income; we use the term "wealthy" to describe the 600,000 or so U.S. households with at least $500,000 in annual discretionary income. The spending power represented by these relative small groups is tremendous. In dollar terms, the 11 million affluent households account for a majority of the assets and consumer spending in the United States.

The Desire to Acquire

"We can do without any article of luxury we have never had; but when once obtained, it is not in human nature to surrender it voluntarily."
—THOMAS CHANDLER HALIBURTON

CHIMPANZEES LIKE PEANUT BUTTER as much as they like frozen juice bars.

That may seem an odd place to begin a book about selling to the affluent. The equivalent preference for two disparate monkey snacks is seemingly far afield from the topic at hand. But in fact, this conclusion about equal primate desires for peanut butter and frozen juice, gleaned from several studies, is actually a useful starting point in understanding a variety of sophisticated human behaviors, including the purchase of luxury products. It turns out that some human behaviors are so deeply ingrained in what we might off-handedly think of as *human nature* that, in fact, they transcend humanity itself. And so it is with the desire to acquire.

As scientists tend to do, primatologist Dr. Sarah Brosnan at Georgia State University introduced an interesting twist to an otherwise well-understood situation. Instead of letting the chimpanzees choose their own snacks, she gave some chimps peanut butter, and then gave them the opportunity to trade their peanut butter for a frozen juice bar. Given the 50/50 preference mentioned, one might expect that half the chimps would make the trade. That is, some might characteristically prefer one over the other, or maybe it would depend on what they were "in the mood for" at the given moment; regardless, the equivalent preference for the two should be consistent. But it's not. In fact, 80 percent chose to keep their peanut butter. The same was true for frozen fruit bars, if a little less dramatically. Handed an icy treat, about 60 percent of the chimps preferred to keep it—again, significantly different from the 50/50 split observed, once "ownership" is taken out of the equation.

It's been called "the endowment effect"—the tendency to value something more when your ownership of it has been established. And as you can see, the phenomenon transcends human behavior; it would appear to be deeply engrained in the DNA of our primate cousins as well. Its impact on human behavior is profound yet subtle. And its effects are observable not just in the scientist's laboratory, but in everyday behavior as well.

When it comes to rounding up participants for psychological research, college students are an even more popular source than chimpanzees. Besides an enthusiasm for free food, chimpanzees and college students share a tendency to display the endowment effect. In fact, replace tubes of peanut butter with chocolate bars, and replace frozen juice bars with coffee mugs, and the behavior of chimps and college students begins to look surprisingly similar (or, perhaps not that surprisingly, depending on how much time you've spent on a college campus). When given a choice of a coffee mug or a chocolate bar, college students express no strong preference for one over the other. But given a chocolate bar, well, good luck if you're in the business of handing out mugs; the students will stick with their chocolate. The opposite is true as well: Given a coffee mug, they prefer to hold on to it, rather than trade it for a supposedly equally desired chocolate bar.

For a while, this element of human (and occasionally nonhuman) behavior seemed poised to upend several tenets of classical economic theory. Built on a "rational actor" model of human behavior, one aspect of economic theory posits that a person's "willingness to pay" for a good should be equal to his or her "willingness to accept" compensation to be deprived of that same good. Debates in academic journals heated up. A flurry of studies dug into the issue in tremendous detail. Some questioned the robustness of the original findings. Others explored the boundaries of the phenomenon, delineating the precise circumstances under which it occurs. But in counterintuitive ways, even these studies seemed to reinforce how "primal" the endowment effect is. Among chimps, for example, the endowment effect occurs with food, but not with "abstract" objects such as rubber bones and knotted ropes. Primatologists believe this means that the power of ownership evolved to help aid survival itself. As Dr. Brosnan put it, "Giving up something that could help with survival or reproduction may have been so risky that it wasn't worth doing even if there was the potential for something better."[1]

Other studies picked apart the fine distinctions between the endowment effect and related phenomena. But again, more often than not, in practical circumstances, these behavioral tendencies likely reinforced the power of the endowment effect, not lessened it. "Loss aversion," for example, is the well-documented tendency to avoid losses more vigorously than seek out gains. That is, losing $5 (or $500,000) is more painful than gaining the same amount is pleasurable. One study reported that when salespeople raise the cost of insurance policies (a painful loss of money from the insured's point of view), consumers are highly motivated to begin price shopping and look to change insurance providers. But when costs are lowered by the same amount (from the consumer's point of view, a gain of money), the impact in terms of improved satisfaction or loyalty is much smaller.[2] Loss aversion may be subtly different from the endowment effect, but in most practical circumstances, the two will work together, making the desire to acquire and the proclivity to accumulate stronger and more prevalent.

Over time, the endowment effect—that curious power of ownership—came to be accepted as one of many "irrationalities" at odds with a perfectly rational representation of human choice (particularly if, as is often done in such discussions, the assumption of rationality is taken to straw-man extremes). The field of behavioral economics emerged as the scientific study of "anomalous" human consumptive behavior; economics broadened in its explanatory power rather than shrank.

While economists struggled to make sense of the seeming irrationality of human behavior, salespeople and marketers embraced it, and they have historically made understanding these quirks a central element of their professions. Consider that staple of infomercial selling—the free trial. Once you own something, you value it more. You get used to it. You embrace its strengths. You begin to look back on your decision to buy (or, more technically, to try with the potential for buying later) with pride in your smarts and resourcefulness. The thought of parting with it is sad and brings to mind all the potential circumstances and consequences of loss. In short, it's loss avoidance and the endowment effect together, with probably a handful of related concepts thrown in (including the desire to avoid the hassles associated with returning products and the reluctance to break what feels like a binding social contract).

Consider the following business-meets-primatology thought experiment. A community of chimpanzees characterized by the free choice of snacks has two products (juice bars and peanut butter), each with 50 percent market share. Senior management at Chimps Ahoy Peanut Butter arm their sales force with free trial packages and a compelling sales pitch: "Just try our peanut butter, Mr. and Mrs. Chimp; if you want to keep it, you can pay me later. And if you decide you want to trade it for a frozen juice bar, just let me know, and I'd be happy to make that trade for you. But I think you'll be really happy about your decision to stick with Chimps Ahoy."

The bottom line is this: People like stuff. They buy stuff. They accumulate stuff. They don't particularly like to get rid of stuff. It is deep in our DNA. It is so primal as to predate humanity itself.

THE ESSENCE OF SELLING: CHANNELING VS. CREATING THE DESIRE TO ACQUIRE

There are, in our opinion, many myths about selling and salespeople, such as:

- A great salesperson can sell anything.

- The best salespeople make the best sales managers.

- Anyone can be turned into a great salesperson.

We'll explore these and other myths in this book, but for now, we tackle one of the biggest: *Salespeople get people to buy things they don't want.*

The desire to acquire is fundamental; the salesperson's role is more about unleashing and channeling that preexisting desire than it is about forcing unwanted items on susceptible prospects. There are, of course, exceptions. Boiler rooms of high-pressure telephone salespeople hocking fraudulent investments do exist. (Speaking of which, anyone reading this book would likely find the movie *Boiler Room* an interesting look at the seedy hard-sell underbelly of the stock brokerage industry. Admittedly imperfect and dramatically flawed as a film—that is, a bit lame—it's worth the viewing not only for its recognizable portrayal of a high-pressure sales environment but also for Ben Affleck's hysterical turn as a low-rent version of Alec Baldwin's coffee-is-for-closers sales guru from *Glengarry Glen Ross*.)

Like so many myths, this one has its origins in commonplace reality, as for generations most salespeople had to close the sale immediately. Peddlers and merchants have been around as long as society has existed, traveling from community to community, seeking to maximize their sales from each person and each town before moving on to the next. They were the traveling Wal-Marts of their day, albeit with smaller selections, and they sought one-shot "transactional" sales. They would be moving on soon, and so they were not focused on building long-term relationships. Their visits were anticipated, their goods were highly sought, and they were one of the biggest distribution channels of the time. But high-pressure tactics were not uncommon, satisfaction after the sale was often low, and the peddlers' reputations suffered as a result. In 1800s America, their numbers boomed, particularly after the Civil War, as former soldiers and waves of new immigrants sought entry-level positions where they could be their own bosses.[3] At the same time, the industrial revolution was increasing the supply of goods, and the return of a peacetime economy was spurring demand. For many, traveling merchant seemed the best path to the American Dream of the time, but the image suffered. These peddlers and merchants were often portrayed in popular culture as swindlers. Jokes were told about dishonest and ineffectual traveling salesmen. Given the frequency with which peddlers called upon farmers in the agrarian society of the day, the jokes often involved a traveling salesman and a farmer's daughter. Admittedly, much of this negative word of mouth was spread by shopkeepers in general stores—direct competitors to the peddlers. Regardless, there seemed to be enough truth in the gossip to perpetuate the image. It's a black eye that continues to endure today.

* * *

Salespeople have a decades-long history of being ranked at the bottom of "Whom do you trust?" survey questions, along with politicians and advertising executives. And as the peddler profession faded away, other sales professionals came to bear the brunt of the antisales sentiment. Perhaps auto dealers have had it worst, and again, there was some kernel of truth that perpetuated the negative stereotypes. After World War II, cars were in short supply; auto factories had been converted to munitions factories and other sources of support for the war effort. At the same time, demand for cars skyrocketed. Soldiers returned home and wartime rationing ended, encouraging consumption of all types. The American Dream evolved with a car soon becoming a central part of it. The emergence of suburbia necessitated the widespread adoption of cars. Soon a luxury was becoming a necessity, but one that retained its position as an emotion-laden aspirational purchase as well.

All of these factors combined in the emergence of a transaction-focused environment. High-pressure sales techniques came along as a result. The simplicity of sticker prices was replaced with complex negotiation; experience and knowledge ensured that the salesperson would have the upper hand. The auto industry developed a bad reputation that remains today, even after the emergence of fixed-price dealerships and an Internet world that has largely corrected the power and information imbalance that once characterized the salesperson-prospect relationship.

But at some level, even boiler rooms and the most nefarious stereotypical car salespersons aren't creating the impulse to purchase; they are simply channeling the desire in their selfish direction via unethical ways. Boiler rooms are selling financial gain, competing against other investments; auto salespeople are trying to win a sale that might otherwise go to the dealership down the street. Particularly when we are talking about affluent individuals and luxury markets, it's less about motivating the desire to purchase and more about winning market share by channeling consumption in the direction of you and your brand.

Again, there are exceptions, particularly when the Great Recession caused consumers both rich and poor to cut back significantly. For example, in 2009, a luxury auto dealership asked us to train its sales associates in dealing with a new phenomenon: prospects deciding to not purchase a car at all. As one salesperson explained it, "I'm losing fewer deals to other dealerships; instead, people are just buttoning their wallet and waiting." But even under extreme circumstances, such as the average affluent person's losing 30 to 40 percent of his or her portfolio at the deepest point of the recession, the decision to not purchase was less common than were value-seeking behaviors. Some put their loyalty to the dealership aside in their quest for a better deal. (Again, to quote one of the sales associates, "Customers who never shopped me before are shopping me now.") Others opened their minds to trading down in quality. ("Nonluxury cars are entering my prospects' consideration set in ways I haven't seen before.")

Even the decision to not purchase was, in actuality, a decision to not purchase *right now*. Before the recession, half of the affluent stated that they "tried to buy a new car every two to three years," but as the recession wore on, that figure dropped to one-third of the affluent. Still, for most, that simply meant a four-year replacement cycle, not a decision to keep their current cars till they pass 100,000 miles.

THE DESIRE TO ACQUIRE . . . SOMETHING NICE

The urge for acquisition is innate and fundamental. So is the urge to acquire something nice. Archeologists often point to the emergence of cave art and symbolic representation as the hallmarks of "fully modern" humans, but much of the earliest art and craftsmanship was in the form of more personal objects—objects that, we can only assume, held deep personal meaning for those who made them: small statues, talismans, jewelry, weaponry crafted with elegance and symbolism that transcended utilitarian need. The list goes on. Today, we might call it luxury, although that word is rife with connotations that may not apply. Acquisition of "luxury" is less about conspicuous consumption and more about owning something of beauty and meaning, of refinement and sophistication. As we shall see, acquisition of luxury means owning or experiencing something exceptional, something created with a true sense of passion and artistry, something that can provide a truly sublime experience. Understanding these motivations is, obviously, crucial to success in selling to today's affluent and wealthy.

The desire for luxury in this sense is nearly universal, and once the cost and availability barriers are brought down, the acquisition of those former luxuries becomes nearly universal as well. Consider the culinary examples. Sugar. Spices such as pepper. Coffee. Chocolate. Silverware. All started out as expensive and rare treats for a select few monarchs and slowly diffused their way through the wealthy aristocracy before eventually entering into mainstream use.

The desire to acquire something nice—luxury, if you will—is so profound that societies have often felt threatened by it and have tried to control it.[4] But in a testament to the power of this desire, those societies have almost always fought a losing battle. In the end, societies usually end up embracing this fundamental human urge. Plato tells of Socrates' admonition that the best life is a simple one, with only what is necessary in terms of clothing and food. ("Many men live to eat; I eat to live.") Further, Plato reasoned, a society in which people conduct themselves in this way will live both peacefully and prosperously. But a "luxurious" society, in which desire and acquisition run amok, he poetically describes as an "inflamed" or "fevered" one. That is, the need to meet society's growing appetite (literally and figuratively) requires ever more resources, ever more territory, more of everything. Plato viewed it as a cultural double-whammy—the aspiration to luxury enhanced the desire to grow territory through warfare, but that same luxurious lifestyle was thought to make people soft, effeminate, even emasculated.

The Greeks were great thinkers. And their thoughts about wealth, luxury, and refinement reverberated through the centuries. The Romans were great doers and lawmakers, and they translated Greek philosophical theory into institutionalized practice. Rome was, of course, home to fabulous and highly concentrated wealth as well as a wholehearted pursuit of "luxury" (although "opulence" and "extravagance" might better capture the spirit of the times). Like Plato, the Roman philosophers preached that the life of desire destroys the individual and destabilizes society. As the Roman poet Juvenal put it,

> *Now all the evils of a long peace are ours;*
> *Luxury, more terrible than hostile powers,*
> *Her baleful influence wide around has hurled*
> *And well avenged the subjugated world.*[5]

Like the Greeks, the Romans also thought a life of luxury had a negative, feminizing effect. But they blamed its presence less on universal human nature and more on the insidious effects of other cultures. Xenophobia ran deep—as Rome conquered more Asian territory, for example, there was fear that the refined "effeminate" sensibility Asians supposedly had toward luxury would infect the troops and return to the Roman homeland with them. In fact, the Romans had such respect for the power of luxurious desires that they even used them as a weapon of war. Tacitus tells that the Roman governor of Britain attempted to calm potentially disruptive townsfolk by getting them hooked on "rest and repose through the charms of luxury." He started with the sons of local chiefs, introducing a lifestyle through which "step by step they were led to things which dispose to vice, the lounge, the bath, the elegant banquet."[6]

The Romans managed their societal fears with a typically institutional approach. The office of the Censor was charged with legislatively managing Roman lifestyles, and when Cato the Elder was elected Censor in 184 BCE, he made stamping out the evils of luxury job number one. In today's terms, high-end products were assessed at very high prices, and luxury taxes were introduced to diminish the enthusiasm for high-end consumption. We might not relate to the currency they used, but the overall approach sure feels familiar: "The assessors were ordered to list jewels and women's dresses and vehicles which were worth more than 15,000 asses at ten times their value . . . and on all of these items a tax of three asses per thousand was to be collected."[7]

Today we'd call this sumptuary legislation, and it is found in the history of many cultures around the world. The English built on the Roman heritage, and in the 1300s they passed laws dictating what kinds of food and clothing were appropriate for each of seven "clauses" of individuals. A "Clause I" person (such as a servant) could wear only the simplest of clothing, while a "Clause V" knight whose lands yielded over 200 pounds could wear clothing worth up to six marks, provided it had fine embroidery. These laws reduced consumption, provided stability to the social structure, and protected domestic merchants from competition from "luxury" providers in other countries.

As Rome fell, luxury took the blame. Sumptuary laws, so the narrative of the time went, were ultimately ineffective, and Rome was dragged down by the pursuit of desire and the supposed weakness and social disruptions thought to result from it. Even the rugged Spartans came to be viewed as having been dragged down by luxury. As the Roman era gave way to the Dark Ages, things got even worse for luxury, going from scapegoat of the Roman decline to the very essence of evil.

The medieval poem *Psychomachia*, for example, describes a grand battle of good versus evil in various guises: Christian Faith versus pagan gods, Chastity versus Lust, Patience versus Anger, and Pride versus Humility. Then Luxuria arrives in a gold- and jewel-encrusted chariot (today it would probably be a bling-encrusted Bentley). She attacks with violets and roses, weakening, effeminizing, seducing even the virtues who won previous rounds of the battle. But Good mounts a comeback, and Temperance arrives to finally kill Luxuria in a scene that would likely guarantee an R-rating if it were faithfully reproduced on the big screen. Still, the point is clear, and the characterization of luxury was cemented for centuries. In fact, Luxuria quite nearly made it to the final list of seven deadly sins, only to be replaced by lust. For centuries, the words "luxury," "lust," "lechery," and "lewdness" became largely interchangeable.

As the Dark Ages gave way to the Renaissance, and free enterprise began to emerge throughout Europe, many influential thinkers began to have a change of heart about luxury. Sure, it could still make individuals weak, they argued, but perhaps it could have positive benefits for society as a whole. After all, highly skilled jobs were created, and a new class of artisans and craftsmen emerged; it was trickle-down economics centuries before that term would be coined. Some began to question whether luxury was really associated with effeminacy; various fighting forces were pointed out to have fought bravely despite an affinity for puffy shirts and powdered wigs. Even the fall of Rome came to be viewed as resulting from poor governance rather than desire run amok.

But the full-fledged rehabilitation of the "desire to acquire" came with Adam Smith, whose book *The Wealth of Nations* would become the intellectual blueprint for the industrial revolution and for modern free enterprise. Central to Adam Smith's thinking was the notion that the desire for improvement was fundamental to human nature—improvement in one's life in general, and in one's material standing in particular. Opulence, in his thinking, was a sign of success, social mobility, and a generally healthy society. Sumptuary laws were unnatural and counterproductive; countries using them were poor and stagnant. In his words, every man was a merchant, motivated by profit and loss. Today we might say that everybody is a salesperson: Regardless of formal profession, everybody is selling something, even if it is just himself or herself. Adam Smith was a nineteenth-century "Gordon

Gecko meets Tony Robbins," combining a "greed is good" attitude with a relentless enthusiasm for self-improvement. Luxury, again in the broad sense of acquiring something sublime, had begun to shed its millennium-long bad rap and was beginning to be appreciated for its positive attributes.

* * *

Acquisition and luxury had found their philosopher in Adam Smith. But just as the Romans implemented the ideas of the Greek thinkers, it would be the French under Louis XIV who would put Smith's philosophy into action, and luxury would begin to take its fully modern form that we would recognize today. Known as the Sun King, he converted Louis XIII's hunting lodge in the Palace at Versailles, and under his 1643–1715 reign, fashion, architecture, interior design, and furniture would all be revisited and rethought with an eye toward an opulence that transcended utility. A few decades later, Marie Antoinette would famously frequent the many purveyors of luxury goods that had sprung up and increasingly come to define the economic culture of Paris. They came to define the psychological culture as well: elite goods reserved for a wealthy few, aspired to by many, but widely resented as well. Reminiscent of the Roman admonition that luxury would destabilize society, the inequalities of the time sparked the French Revolution, and although Marie Antoinette didn't survive it, surprisingly the enthusiasm for luxury largely did. Within less than seventy-five years after the egalitarian-striving revolutionary upheaval, a new breed of merchants built on this surviving enthusiasm for luxury and opened businesses in Paris. Many of the names we still recognize today: Hermès, Cartier, Louis Vuitton. The desire to acquire, both the everyday and the refined, is deep and resilient, indeed.

SO WHAT'S THE PROBLEM?
THE BIGGEST CHALLENGE IN SALES TODAY

The biggest challenge in sales today is not a lack of consumer desire. Indeed, our brief review of history shows that the desire to acquire extends beyond human nature, and has rarely been stamped out, despite many attempts by many societies. It has been a challenge for governments seeking to maintain the status quo, and for philosophers who feared that luxury would destroy the moral fabric of society. But for merchants, marketers, and salespeople, greater challenges lie elsewhere. Even as the economic downturn of the later 2000s drags into a new decade, the desire to acquire remains profound and fundamental. More restrained than in 2005 or 2006, to be sure, but as we have seen, it is still there and still powerful.

The biggest challenge in sales today, particularly as it pertains to the affluent, is this: *Customers have stopped listening*. In increasing numbers, affluent consumers have stopped seeking out salespeople. They rely on salespeople less. They increasingly go to the Internet to avoid salespeople altogether.

Why? The unfortunate truth is that most salespeople aren't very good. The promise of a great sales experience is remembered fondly from the past, but it is being fulfilled with increasing rarity today. For example, in 2007, our annual *Survey of Affluence and Wealth in America*, produced with American Express Publishing, found that two-thirds of the affluent agreed with the statement: "I depend on the salesperson to know the specific details of a product that makes it worth more." By 2010, that figure had dropped to 49 percent. In 2007, 39 percent agreed with the statement: "I have close relationships with a few salespeople that I count on," a figure that dropped to 25 percent by 2010.

Our 2010 *Affluent Attitudes Toward Salespeople* survey, conducted among consumers earning more than $125,000 per year, led to similar conclusions about the declining influence of salespeople (see Table 1.1). Slightly more than nine in ten customers have largely made up their minds about what they want—and what they'll pay—before a salesperson enters the equation. Nearly as many agree that a true sales professional is hard to find, and that salespeople are less influential in their purchase decisions than they used to be. On the whole, today's salespeople are viewed as order takers who simply aren't as knowledgeable or as skilled as salespeople in the past. The result is that most people would rather avoid interacting with the salesperson completely, preferring to shop on the Internet when possible and wanting to be left alone when they do venture into a retail store.

TABLE 1.1

Attitudes of Affluent Buyers Toward Salespeople

Statement	% in Agreement
When purchasing luxury or high-end products and services, I usually know what I want and what I'm willing to pay for it before interacting with a salesperson.	94%
A true sales professional is hard to find.	90
I rely less on salespeople today than in the past when making purchase decisions.	85
I prefer to be left alone while I'm shopping at a retail store.	85
Salespeople today are mainly order takers and transaction facilitators.	71
Salespeople today aren't as good as salespeople were 10 or 20 years ago.	67
When possible, I'd prefer to buy things on the Internet and avoid salespeople altogether.	67
I'd be proud to have my child (or other close relative) become a sales professional.	48

Source: *Affluent Attitudes Toward Salespeople*, survey conducted by Harrison Group, 2010.

USING THE THREE PASSIONS
TO ACHIEVE SALES SUCCESS

Our research not only has revealed widespread dissatisfaction with the state of sales today but also has explored the opposite side of the equation. That is, we have studied excellence. We've developed training programs for selling $1,000 fashion accessories, $5,000 suits, and $10,000 handbags; $100,000 automobiles; $1 million pieces of jewelry and $5 million homes; $10 million private jets, and investment services for those with $50 million. At each stop, we interviewed the top performers to learn their best practices, and we helped hone their skills. We've helped them find more qualified prospects, increase their conversion rates, and drive business growth. We've helped many salespeople become wealthy themselves, but, even more important, become happier and more fulfilled in their jobs.

We have also studied hundreds of mutually satisfying interactions between salespeople and customers. The best of these interactions—those that are meaningful to customers and profitable for companies—are consistently characterized by three distinct sets of passions. Each is a story rife with lessons for anyone in any profession who aspires to achieve more. But understanding the three passions is not a nice-to-have, cherry-on-top self-help gift you'll get from this book. Instead, understanding these three passions is fundamental to reengaging interest in working with salespeople (see Figure 1.1). It is fundamental to answering the question at hand: *How does one more effectively sell to affluent individuals?*

FIGURE 1.1

The Three Passions for Sales Success

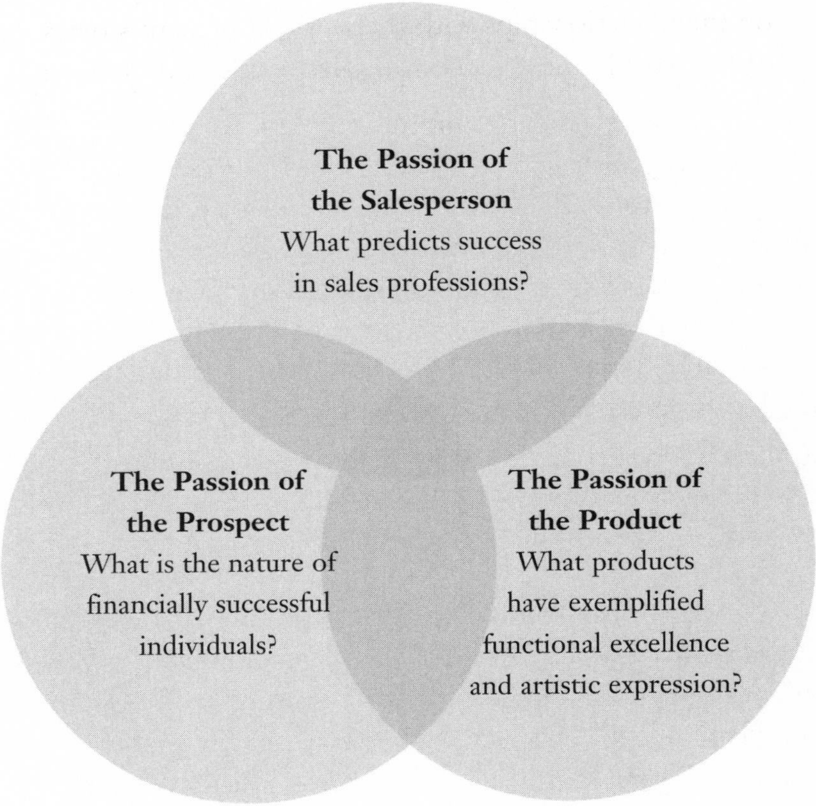

**The Passion of
the Salesperson**
What predicts success
in sales professions?

**The Passion of
the Prospect**
What is the nature of
financially successful
individuals?

**The Passion of
the Product**
What products
have exemplified
functional excellence
and artistic expression?

1. *The Passion of the Salesperson.* Sales success comes not to
   dabblers and dilettantes but to those with a true love
   of what they do. They have found that having a sales
   position fits well with their interests and goals, and they
   have customized that position to suit their style. Success

comes to them in part because they are so happy doing what they do; similarly, prospects are happy to interact with them and feel good about spending money based on their relationships with them. We'll present stories of the world's most successful salespeople and discover that the "secrets" to their sales successes transfer readily to other professions and domains of life.

2. *The Passion of the Prospect.* Our research has found that most wealthy individuals became wealthy not by aspiring to wealth per se but by pursuing a personal passion. They came from middle-class backgrounds, worked hard, and achieved financial success through corporate leadership or entrepreneurship. Over 90 percent created their own wealth. The results are prospects with middle-class mindsets and a strong value orientation that has intensified with the economic downturn, creating obvious challenges for salespeople. But these prospects understand a sales appeal based on passion; they respect people who have passions; and most important, under the right circumstances, they are willing to pay for expressions of passion.

3. *The Passion of the Product.* In most product and service categories, there is a quality and price level far above the mainstream offerings. This is luxury—the point at which details transcend mere excellence to create a sublime emotional resonance. These details might be in the materials, or in the history of the brand, or in the craftsmanship or design; the luxury product has

been created with a passion that exceeds utilitarian need and expresses true emotion for the product. Similarly, service, and luxury service in particular, is delivered in a manner that surprises and delights, and that brings about an emotional response that exceeds practical need. We'll explore the stories behind some of the world's unique and exquisite products—those that have stood the test of time as exemplars of functional excellence and artistic expression—and identify how the passion implicit within them is in fact the key to selling them.

In the next three chapters, we explore these passions—these areas of success—that characterize the most mutually satisfying interactions between salespeople and their customers. Then, in the chapters that follow, we explore easy, effective, proven ways to bring these three passions together in the selling context.

CHAPTER TWO

The
Passion of the
Salesperson

"Nothing great in the world has ever been accomplished without passion."
—**GEORG WILHELM FRIEDRICH HEGEL**

"Desire is the starting point of all achievement, not a hope, not a wish, but a keen pulsating desire, which transcends everything."
—**NAPOLEON HILL**

"There is no passion to be found playing small—in settling for a life that is less than the one you are capable of living."
—**NELSON MANDELA**

WE'VE INTERVIEWED AND TRAINED hundreds of successful salespeople who make their livelihood by building relationships with wealthy individuals. The first and most obvious impression one gets of these top performers is that they have, for a lack of a better phrase, a sense of passion.

Let's not let semantics get in the way. If, for you, what we are talking about is not passion, then choose your own word: *Drive. Hunger. Persistence. Determination. Tenacity. Relentlessness. Focus. Intensity. Proactivity.* Or, choose your cliché to describe these individuals: "They take the bull by the horns." "They get it done." "They make their own luck." "They have a fire in the belly." "They are positive thinkers." "They don't take no for an answer."

A PASSION FOR SALES

In some top salespeople, the passion for sales manifests itself as a quiet confidence or a steely determination. This archetype is found throughout the research, history, and mythology of sales success. For example, thirty-five years before Ross Perot's focused, unblinking gaze caught the nation's attention during his presidential run, he used that determination to become one of the greatest salesmen in IBM's history. In his final year with the company, he achieved his annual sales goal by January 19. Or so the story goes. And it's a good story, often retold, with Perot achieving unofficial hall-of-fame status in the competitive world of sales.

How Perot might have managed such a feat is probably unknowable at this point. *Time* investigated the claim during

Perot's 1992 presidential campaign, interviewing more than twenty of Perot's colleagues from his IBM days, but the magazine was forced to concede: "Some of their memories are fading, a number of key players are dead, and documents are virtually nonexistent."[1] It's clear, though, that he wasn't widely liked, with descriptions of Perot ranging from "immoral," to a more politically correct "not a team player," to a more charitable "He was practicing '80s ethics in the 1960s." He likely wouldn't disagree; he once described his "role in life is that of the grain of sand to the oyster—it irritates the oyster and out comes a pearl."[2]

Regardless of the story's validity, it's clear that Ross Perot was widely respected for his sales ability—and his drive, in particular. One colleague summed it up this way: "I still don't like him . . . but I've never seen anybody who could accomplish as much as this son of a gun could." In 1962, Perot left his five-year stint at IBM to start Electronic Data Systems (EDS), and (possibly apocryphal sales story no. 2) had his sales pitches rejected seventy-nine times before he landed his first client. But, mythology aside, it's clear that Perot's drive was truly exceptional and he got inarguable results. EDS went public within just six years of its founding, with its stock price rising from $16 to $160 within days of its Initial Public Offering, launching Perot from the ranks of millionaires to the ranks of billionaires. He never tempered his style. Soon after selling EDS to General Motors for over $2.4 billion (in 1984), he became a vocal critic of GM's quality, concluding that "revitalizing GM is like teaching an elephant to tap dance. You find the sensitive parts and start poking."[3]

Whether you like Ross Perot or not doesn't matter. We are not putting him on a pedestal or holding him up as an ideal. Instead, he's offered here as the archetype—the highly successful salesperson, driven by his passion for sales. He's relentless, determined, and—to use our word—passionate. Sometimes to a fault.

This same image of a relentless, driven person is found repeatedly in the world of sales, and among entrepreneurs more generally. Think of Donald Trump. Mark Cuban. Boardwalk barkers cum infomercial screamers such as the late Billy Mays. The persona is at the core of the sales-motivation subculture, in which Tony Robbins is merely the best known member. Dozens of sales gurus have dedicated followings of various sizes, and their followers collectively spend millions of dollars on books, audio programs, and seminars meant to help them enhance sales performance.

There is always an underlying truth to archetypes and mythology, even if the details don't always hold up to scientific scrutiny. (Comedian Stephen Colbert's concept of "truthiness" comes to mind: a form of truth known intuitively "from the gut, not books," without regard to evidence or logical examination.) And there is certainly profound truth to the notion of passion being at the core of sales success. As the following two case studies show, this particular truth is widely supported by both research and experience.

CASE STUDY
Top Sales Performers on Fifth Avenue

We've heard about the power of passion virtually every time we've interviewed top performers. For example, we developed a training program for sales associates and personal shoppers at one of the world's most prestigious luxury retail stores. It's the kind of store that piqued Carrie Bradshaw's enthusiasm on *Sex and the City*. While the elite clientele varies throughout the day, the store's patrons are consistent in having large wallets and high standards. These ladies who lunch pop in en masse at midday, and a small fashion posse of them collectively might spend six figures. Likewise, CEOs visit after work for $10,000 suits. After hours, VIPs with special security concerns are brought in for shopping sprees that range into the millions: Saudi royalty one night, international celebrities the next.

We started our interviews with the best sales associates and personal shoppers—those whose commission-based compensation is well into the six figures. We asked them about the secret of their success in retail sales. First, we needed to coax them past any objections they may have had to the word *success*; their modesty is consistent with the modesty we often see in successful individuals across professions, sales or not. But there was method to our madness. Getting people to talk about their professional successes is a powerful way to start an interview; it is flattering, of course, but it also engages their curiosity. We have often said that our biggest research challenge is finding successful salespeople and wealthy individuals willing to be interviewed. Our second biggest is getting them to stop talking once we've started the interview.

Our interviews often start with questions about the reasons for their success, and they often lead to the same answer: the passion thing. We've often heard about the effort, and the attitude, and the hunger, and it features in these interviews.

- "Hunger. Drive. Desire."

- "It's not about opening a door. Anybody can do that. You really have to work it."

- "Really putting in the hours and the effort. Being productive during downtime."

- "I see a lot of standing around, and I just say to myself: 'My God, there is so much to be done!'"

- "I go the extra mile. I put a lot of effort in. I follow up. I stay in touch."

- "I ended up building my business in my quiet times. I realized that I had to reach out, instead of just standing there waiting for business to walk in."

- "I'm always busy. I'm calling. I'm sending notes. I will call and say I'm putting together a little package. I will e-mail clients I haven't heard from in a month or two. I'll send them a little something for their birthday, or grandkids being born, or bar mitzvahs.

If somebody has a benefit, I'll have the store give a gift certificate. The list goes on."

We spoke to the store's vice president responsible for all the sales associates and personal shoppers, including the hiring and firing. As in many sales organizations, the company brings in many entry-level individuals, a handful of whom rise to elite heights and some of whom underachieve and leave quickly. The cost to the store is considerable (time and money wasted on hiring and training), and the cost to the unsuccessful associate is considerable as well (wasted time and an unnecessary emotional toll). But through experience and research, the recruiting process at this store has become a refined and targeted effort to recruit, hire, and foster the growth of those most likely to succeed. As our vice president put it, she looks for:

> *"Someone who really has a passion for what they do. It has to be more than: 'I love to be around people. . . . I love to be around clothing.' When I interview somebody who says that to me, I have red flags that go up. Yeah, we all love to be around people and clothing—that's why we do what we do. But there's got to be something else . . . there's got to be an edge. Being personable. Being organized. Understanding that you are a businessperson and knowing how you are running your business. Thinking outside the box to take yourself to the next level. Getting all the knowledge you need—not just standing by a register and thinking the traffic is going to come to you. Knowing what's going on in the world, and relating that back to*

what you do. Somebody who is a go-getter. Somebody who says: 'This is it. This is what I want.' Not somebody who sees it as a 9-to-5 job, but somebody who sees it as a career path. Someone who understands what clientele-ing is all about, and what our store is all about in terms of customer standards, and so on."

CASE STUDY

Top Sales Performers in a
Dallas Luxury Auto Dealership

Different company, different industry, different location— but remarkably similar insights into what determines success. As with the previous case study, we interviewed top performers, this time at one of the most successful luxury automobile dealerships in America, to hear their secrets of success. Here's what they had to say:

- "First, make sure this is what you want to do. Think about what kind of person you want to be. It's less about making money, and more about your own personal development. If you are just dabbling, don't do it."

- "Sometimes new people say, 'Oh, look at her . . . she just works 9 to 6. Must be nice.' I don't work 9 to 6. They don't see me at home working at 10 or 11 at night. I'm up at 5 every morning on the computer. You're not going to make $100,000 your first year working 9 to 5. I didn't build my business in a year."

- "Networking was *huge* for me when I started. It's so important not to sit here and wait for people to come through the door. It's just not going to happen. You have to get out there and build relationships. Find something you enjoy with those people—then just get out there and connect."

- "You've got to give it your best. You've got to think positive. You've got to go after it. Every morning, you have to have the mindset: 'I can sell something today.' If you're not going to do that, you might as well take the day off."

A PASSION FOR RELATIONSHIPS

Aside from having a passion for selling, another characteristic of highly successful salespeople is their passion for relationships. That doesn't necessarily mean that they are extraverts or the life of the party. But they have and show an interest in the lives of others. It's an intellectual interest, to be sure, with many salespeople being "armchair psychologists" who have read about or observed human behavior, particularly as it relates to sales and persuasion. But it is also a sincere and practical interest; they care about people.

Building relationships is the essence of successful sales. The goal is to turn that person who is a onetime sale into a repeat customer. And having a passion for developing relationships is key to making that change. Top sales performers confirm this:

- "The secret in luxury sales is to develop a following. You meet someone, and you give them such great service that the experience sticks with them, and the customer sticks with you."

- "Top performers aren't just concerned about the initial sale. They ask: 'How do I form a relationship? How do I get their repeat business?'"

- "When I see a new piece come in, I ask myself: 'Who could that be for?' I don't wait for the customer to come to me."

One of the very best, a retail salesperson generating an income well into the six-figure range, summed it up well:

> *[Top performers] aren't just focused on taking it and ringing it. They are truly interacting with clients. Mediocre performers are just clerking sales or ringing sales, instead of finding out: 'How can I get this client to come back?' Top performers aren't just concerned about this initial sale. They ask: 'How do I form a relationship? How do I get their repeat business?' Because that's really where the business is and where the money gets made. It's not about taking this one sale—that one sale could come back. 'How do I connect with this client to make her want to work with me again? How can I make her OK with me calling her again, sending her photos of new merchandise, etc.?*

How do I start that relationship?' The associate that takes that extra step—that isn't just happy with this one sale—that associate is the one who wins in the end, because that is the associate that clients want to work with."

THE LONG HISTORY OF PASSION-BASED SELLING

That passion stands at the core of sales success is both a very old and a very new notion. Before there were brick-and-mortar bookstores and community libraries, and long before there was the Internet, publishers hired peddlers to sell their books. Bible societies in particular had large sales forces, many of whom were known for their fervor; they were, after all, selling not merely books but also salvation—in their minds, they were literally selling the very word of God. Ebeneezer Hannaford's *Success in Canvassing: A Practical Manual of Hints and Instructions, Specifically Adapted to the Use of Book Canvassers of the Better Class*, published in 1875, preached the importance of persistence, hard work, and passion as essential to selling (even presenting topics in military terms, with chapter titles such as "Organizing for Victory" and "Opening the Campaign").[4] Similarly, snake oil salesmen were known for their impassioned sales pitches. The main character in Abraham Cahan's 1917 book *The Rise of David Levinsky* says: "I developed into a successful salesman. If I were asked to name some single element of my success on

43

the road, I should mention the enthusiasm with which I usually spoke of my merchandise. It was genuine, and it was contagious. Retailers could not help believing that I believed in my goods."[5]

The idea of passion is a thread that continues to run through sales today. Og Mandingo's 1968 book *The Greatest Salesman in the World*, which continues to be widely read today, gives the simple message: "do it now." In his 2005 book *The Art of Selling to the Affluent*, Matt Oechsli concludes that commandment number 1 is to "be totally committed."[6] When author Remy Stern interviewed Ron Popeil, the infomercial king whose autobiography is modestly titled *The Salesman of the Century*, he was struck by the obviousness of Popeil's two great loves—cooking and selling. Popeil's kitchen includes a floor-to-ceiling bookcase with "every sauce, condiment, and marinade imaginable," as well as what he claims is one of the world's largest collections of olive oil. And as for his passion for selling, Popeil has a professional video camera, a tripod, and a stack of videotapes, including tapes of him practicing infomercial pitches at all hours of the day and night.[7]

The Rise of Scientific Management

Although this idea of passion has been engrained in sales from its very beginning, it can be hard to quantify, predict, and systematize. As a result, passion took a backseat in thinking about sales success for several generations. The shift started with a movement known as *scientific management*, an attempt to bring rigor to the challenging task of managing growing organizations in the early era of mass production and marketing. Managers would carefully study individuals at work, break their efforts down into the smallest possible behaviors, and then install systems to teach those behaviors in great detail. Managerial control was crucial; individuality was an error in the system to be stamped out.

Frederick W. Taylor's 1911 *The Principles of Scientific Management* was the bible of the movement, but the basic ideas had been percolating for decades, since the dawn of the industrial revolution. It wasn't long before companies with large sales forces began applying these ideas to the previously wild, wooly, and radically idiosyncratic world of sales. In *Scientific Sales Management: A Practical Application of the Principles of Scientific Management to Selling*, Charles Wilson Hoyt wrote:

> Scientific Sales Management believes in the proper training of the salesman. This training even goes down to the individual motions and work of the salesman. It goes so far as to insist upon the substitution of exact methods of work by the individual salesman for scattered efforts. This is carried out even to the matter of standardizing, in some propositions, the salesman's talk, his manner of approach, etc.[8]

Perhaps the best known popularizer of these ideas was John Patterson of National Cash Register, whose huge sales force called on growing businesses around the country. He was certainly a believer in the role of passion in sales. The company newsletter, *The Salesman*, ran with the subtitle "Our Password: Hustle." He sponsored motivational sales conferences. He paid high commissions to keep their energy up. He wrote:

> A sickly, nervous man cannot exert that personal magnetism which unconsciously cuts such a large figure in the success of every salesman. Not only the practical manager of the sales department of every large corporation, but as well the professors who write on the psychology of salesmanship, insist that good health and abundant animal spirits are perhaps the most important qualifications a salesman can have for his work.[9]

"Abundant animal spirits" is certainly the most unique metaphor for passion we've come across in the sales literature, but it makes the point.

Despite his belief in passion, his even stronger belief in the "scientific" approach to sales meant putting systems and consistent terminology into place, much of which still exists in actuality or in spirit today. Daily reports on sales and prospecting submitted by 8:15 A.M. Monthly quotas overseen by sales managers, who met to review sales figures each

Monday at 8 A.M. Sales scripts. Prepared answers for countering common objections. Persuasion techniques such as frequently asking questions guaranteed to get prospects to repeatedly say yes, or handing them a pen to push them toward signing a purchase order, or asking, "What color do you want?" rather than "Do you want it?" Expecting salespeople to "hustle collections as hard as they hustle for orders." A four-step sales process: approach, proposition, demonstration, and close. A sales training school taught it all. There were clubs and awards for those making their quotas. There were sales-as-warfare analogies and calls to military discipline; Patterson said, "I believe that a business ought to be like a battleship in many respects—in cleanliness, in order, in the perfect discipline of the men."[10] Patterson's ideas were massively influential. Over time, many of his senior managers left for other firms, spreading ideas about scientific sales management throughout the corporate landscape. There was one "right way" to do it. Success lay in the system, not in the individual.

Predicting Success in Sales:
Common Knowledge ≠ Compelling Results

The challenge is that a century of this rah-rah conclusion about the power of passion, when compared to the research findings, begins to look tenuous, or at least overly simplistic, or perhaps just plain wrong. The literature on sales performance is large, with studies of sales performance appearing as early as 1918.[11] But even decades of research seem to have yielded underwhelming results; a lack of a consistency in methods and metrics has made clear-cut conclusions difficult to obtain. In the 1980s, scientists developed ways of integrating quantitative research from a variety of studies. Called meta-analysis—literally, the analysis of analyses—these techniques allowed researchers to draw conclusions from the voluminous, if maddeningly unsatisfying, research that had been done on salesperson effectiveness.

In the mid-1980s, four business-school professors picked up the gauntlet and attempted to locate every published quantitative study of salesperson effectiveness.[12] They combed through hundreds of studies, whittling down the list to the 116 most methodologically sophisticated. Beginning with the 1918 study, they analyzed studies that spanned decades and constituted an enormous collective sample. The professors concluded that the average correlation between actual sales performance and a hypothesized driver of sales performance is .18.

Let's take a moment and put that finding into perspective. A correlation of zero means that there is no relationship between two variables. A correlation of 1.0 reflects a perfect one-to-one association between two variables—the flawless prediction of one variable from another. (Not surprisingly, a correlation of 1.0 is rarely seen in actual research.) Historically, statisticians squared correlations, multiplying them by themselves to explain the "proportion of variance accounted for." Using this guideline, the variables that the researchers had used to predict sales success had accounted for only 4 percent of the variance in how salespeople actually performed—a dismal showing. The professors, explicitly disheartened, were forced to conclude: "The generally small size of the correlations between predictors and performance criteria is somewhat discouraging."[13] Today's guidelines for interpreting correlations in scientific and market research are more charitable, but they still put a correlation of .18 in the small to moderate range. That is, correlations of .10 are generally considered as small, .3 as moderate, and .5 as large.[14] (Correlations in the .80 range are considered as "reliability coefficients," reflecting that the same underlying construct has been measured in two different ways.)

It's not so much the low average correlation of .18 that's discouraging, however; after all, it's an average, and there were individual studies that stood out in the group as being more on the trail of identifying a profound effect. But the correlations didn't increase over time, suggesting that research findings and theoretical advancement hadn't been able to improve the ability to predict who would succeed and who would not. And it was discouraging to find such low correlations from measures specifically designed to predict sales performance, and many merely seem restatements of being an effective salesperson (see Table 2.1). A test designed to be a measure of salesperson skill or aptitude, for example, that correlates only .2 with actual performance is not particularly something to write home about.

TABLE 2.1
Predictors of Sales Performance

Type of Predictor	Average Correlation
Role (how the salesperson perceives the job and responsibilities)	.30
Skill (as a salesperson)	.28
Motivation	.23
Aptitude (tests specifically designed to measure aptitude for sales)	.17
Personal factors (such as age, gender)	.17
Environmental factors (such as compensation structure and organizational culture)	.14
Average	.18

Source: Churchill et al., "The Determinants of Salesperson Performance: A Meta-Analysis," *Journal of Marketing Research* 22 (May 1985): 103–18.

The unfortunate fact is that most investigations into determinants of sales excellence have yielded the same lukewarm results. A 2005 meta-analysis of fifty-one studies found that commitment to the organization predicts sales performance, with an average correlation of—you guessed it—the same low to middling .18 revealed by the other research.[15] And again, consider the intuitive nature of the finding: Salespeople who like the organization they work for, and have an emotional commitment to it, outsell those who don't—but only modestly.

Even more discouraging are the results from research that has attempted to connect sales performance with more "distant" variables, which would be less restatements of the seemingly obvious and more meaningful information. Literally decades of research on personality traits have been synthesized into "the Big Five"—five core dimensions of personality that have been identified consistently in research over time and across cultures: extraversion, agreeableness, conscientiousness, emotional stability, and openness to experience. Two of these dimensions consistently predict strong sales performance, but the correlations are even smaller than before.[16] *Conscientiousness*, as measured by Big Five tests, refers to the tendency to be organized, responsible, and dependable. Studies have shown conscientiousness to be associated with hard work, determination, and being goal oriented. Surely such a personality trait would correlate highly to success in a field like sales, which often requires a self-starter who can win the trust of prospects. And it does, in the modest .10 to .20 range of variables we explored earlier. And it doesn't just predict sales success—it has the same modest predictive power over success among midlevel managers, police officers, and semiskilled laborers. Ditto *extraversion*—the tendency to be outgoing and active—which correlates an even more modest .10 to .15 with sales success. There's essentially no correlation at all between sales performance and openness to experience, agreeableness, likeability, or emotional stability.

In short, the research shows that sales excellence is not about being male or female, young or old, likeable or cranky, cultured or crude, stable or neurotic. Successful salespeople are ever so slightly more likely to be extraverted or conscientious, but there are plenty of people in sales who are introverted or undependable. Either way, it helps if they are committed to their organizations.

Interesting? Yes. Helpful to a salesperson or a sales manager? Maybe a little. The key to sales success? Not really.

Optimism and the Pinpointing of Passion

Amid research with seemingly middling or inconsistent results, there are, nevertheless, several lines of research that converge on the central role of passion and related ideas in sales success.

One of the most notable efforts was conducted by University of Pennsylvania psychologist Martin Seligman for the Metropolitan Life Insurance Company in the 1980s.[17] Known today as the father of positive psychology (the scientific study of happy, highly achieving people), Seligman was best known at the time as the leading researcher in human optimism. He was approached by Metropolitan Life, an industry behemoth in the 1950s that had seen its market position, and its sales force, erode over the decades. As the company had explored alternative channels of distribution, the sales force dropped from 20,000 to just 8,000 and became less effective as well. Met Life was losing $75 million a year hiring agents who would turn out to be ineffective and eventually leave. A lot of agents, in fact—5,000 a year—had been carefully screened from a pool of over 60,000. Yet half of them were quitting in the first year; 80 percent quit by their fourth year. Only a small percentage turned out to be top performers. And Met Life certainly wasn't alone; turnover has been, and continues to be, a major problem among salespeople in the life insurance industry. But the company's weak market position made the problem particularly pressing, and so Met life sought out Seligman to explore how an understanding of optimism might enhance the effectiveness of its sales force.

The research results were clear: Optimists outsold pessimists. By a lot. In one study, optimistic life insurance agents outsold pessimistic ones by 8 percent in the first year, expanding to 31 percent by the second year, as the power of passion and persistence began to shine through more dramatically. Follow-up studies suggested that the impact of optimism on sales performance could be even greater, particularly in the high-rejection cold-calling environment typical at the time. After nine calls and nine rejections, the optimist thinks, "The tenth call could be my next sale." After nine calls and nine rejections, the pessimist thinks, "My life sucks." For the latter, a cycle of avoidance and procrastination begins, spiraling into passivity and burnout. As a result of Seligman's research, Met Life rethought its approach to hiring and training and saw its sales force and market share grow dramatically.

In fact, the 1980s and 1990s saw growing bodies of research addressing the emotional and motivational elements of sales performance. A 1998 meta-analysis on the predictors of sales excellence examined 129 studies and confirmed the modest correlations with the Big Five personality traits we described.[18] But the researchers uncovered some tantalizing clues to stronger relationships as well. They divided extraversion into two subdimensions: affiliation and potency. *Affiliation* refers purely to one's sociability, while *potency* refers to one's impact, influence, and energy in social interactions. The studies showed that affiliation had a small impact on sales performance, but potency had a much stronger impact, with correlations in the .26 to .28 range. The researchers also divided conscientiousness into two subdimensions: dependability and achievement. *Dependability* had only a small impact on sales performance, while *achieve-*

ment was a more influential dimension, with correlations from .25 to .41, suggesting that striving for competence plays a greater role in sales success.

But the biggest predictor this research uncovered was not a personality trait but, rather, a variable they labeled simply as "interest in sales," which correlated a substantial .50 with both sales managers' perceptions of their sales staff and actual sales performance. (In contrast, salespeople high in "general cognitive ability"—in other words, smarts—were rated more highly by sales managers but they didn't sell any better than their less "cognitively able" counterparts.) The predictive power in what the researchers rather mundanely labeled as "interest in sales" is both intuitive and revealing. And although it doesn't literally use the word *passion*, clearly the conclusion is the same.

The case is similar for the deservedly popular research on sales effectiveness conducted by the well-known polling firm Gallup. Its signature concept, which it considers to be at the heart of excellent corporate performance (sales and otherwise), is *strengths*. Simply put, different salespeople have different strengths: Some are competitive, others are relationship focused, still others are excellent learners or listeners, and so on. Top sales performance, Gallup argues, is not associated with any strength in particular; instead, it comes from understanding and leveraging one's existing strengths. The Gallup concept is more process focused and less content driven than our notion of passions, but the parallels are obvious and the conclusions are highly similar. Consider some of the take-aways from Gallup's research, such as the role of passion as driving sales success: "Our research indicates that the happier you feel about your performance and the greater your satisfaction in your sales role, the more your customers will want to buy from you."[19] On discovering one's passions and molding one's environment: "The best salespeople adapt that job to suit their strengths; they do not attempt to change their strengths to suit their job."[20] On people who don't play to their strengths: "[They] dread going to work . . . treat customers poorly . . . achieve less on a daily basis."[21]

The Gallup research suggests that the end result of a job in which one can effectively pursue one's strengths is "engagement." Employee engagement is a strong predictor of sales performance, employee profitability, customer focus, company loyalty, and even workplace safety. The problem with employee engagement, or playing to your strengths, or pursuing your passions, or whatever language you want to use is that *not enough people do it*. In worldwide research with more than 10 million employees, Gallup discovered that only one in three strongly agreed with the statement: "At work, I have the opportunity to do what I do best every day." Using a similar model, consultancy BlessingWhite concluded that only 29 percent of employees worldwide are fully engaged and 19 percent are actively disengaged (e.g., actively spreading their discontentment), with the majority stuck in something of a blah middle ground.[22] The impact on the bottom line is clear: Outstanding companies average more than nine times as many engaged employees as unengaged ones, whereas average companies have a ratio of less than two-to-one.[23]

So what's the conclusion? It is easy to see why the affluent are pulling back from salespeople. In most circumstances, they have only a one-in-three chance of getting a salesperson who is passionate about what he or she is doing!

LIFESTYLES OF SUCCESSFUL SALESPEOPLE

Who are successful salespeople, and what are they like on a day-to-day basis? A complementary look at successful salespeople, and additional insights into their success, come from our ongoing *Survey of Affluence and Wealth in America* (produced jointly with American Express Publishing, and described more fully in the appendix). For the past five years, we have surveyed Americans with at least $100,000 in annual discretionary income, including many with incomes well over $1 million. This survey provides a broad representative look at the affluent and wealthy populations in the United States. But for now, let's examine a subset of the respondents: the roughly 5 percent who describe themselves as sales and marketing executives. They are successful indeed, averaging over $420,000 in annual income and $3 million in liquid assets. We compare them not to less successful salespeople but, rather, to other affluent individuals who have achieved a similar level of financial success in fields other than sales (see Table 2.2).

TABLE 2.2
Self-Descriptors of Successful Salespeople

% Describing Themselves as . . .	Total	
	Affluent Population	Affluent Salespeople
Intelligent	84%	80%
Loyal	79	78
Family-focused	74	76
Competitive	53	**72**
Driven to succeed	44	**57**
Athletic	32	**47**
Winner	34	**45**
Spiritual	35	**44**
Patient	**48**	38

Source: Harrison Group and American Express Publishing, *Survey of Affluence and Wealth in America*, 2010.

First, we see that the three most commonly used self-descriptors—intelligent, loyal, and family-focused—are consistent among salespeople and those in other professions. But the broader pattern of results reveals the characteristics of sales success that we have shed light on. Salespeople are far more likely to describe themselves as competitive, driven to succeed, and winners, and less likely to describe themselves as patient. They are also more likely to describe themselves as spiritual—perhaps a surprising finding, but we have heard this in our qualitative interviews as well. For some, a sales career can become an expression of their spiritual focus and their desire to serve others. Academic research has also found that religious people tend to be happier, and happy people are generally more successful, for a variety of reasons.[24]

Salespeople are also more likely to describe themselves as athletic; this may reflect their sense of competitiveness as expressed in other domains, although it may play a more direct role as well, as exercise is associated with persistence, goal accomplishment, stress reduction, and overall mood. Their interest in sports is extensive and wide ranging, including firsthand participation, television viewing, and attendance at sporting events (see Table 2.3). Their profile of preferred activities also reveals that, at the risk of reaffirming stereotypes, salespeople are slightly more likely to regularly drink alcoholic beverages (50 percent vs. 43 percent), gamble (24 percent vs. 17 percent), and play golf (9.6 average rounds per year vs. 6.6). The stereotype of the frequently traveling

TABLE 2.3
Leisure Activities of Top Salespeople

Regularly . . .	Total	
	Affluent Population	Affluent Salespeople
Watch sports on TV	46%	60%
Watch ESPN	33	47
Attend live sporting events	34	46
Swim	23	31
Go biking	20	27
Go boating/sailing	15	22

Source: Harrison Group and American Express Publishing, *Survey of Affluence and Wealth in America*, 2010.

salesperson is safe as well. They average sixteen to seventeen nights in hotels annually for vacations, just like their non-sales counterparts, but they average 10.5 business trips a year with over twenty-three nights spent in hotels compared to averages of 4.9 business trips and 12.5 business hotel stays for the affluent population as a whole.

DISCOVER YOUR PASSION AND MOLD YOUR ENVIRONMENT

Your personal sales success is about discovering the passion within you and choosing and molding your environment to fit that passion. It's about finding ways to express that passion that fit with your personal style.

Passion transcends personal style. In fact, it morphs and manifests itself differently in different people, depending on personal style. When we interviewed top performers at the luxury auto dealership described earlier in this chapter, we were struck by the variety of passions that could be expressed through top sales performance. One person simply had a passion for winning, for topping the company sales charts each year. Another had a passion for the Internet and had built a thriving customer base through savvy search-engine optimization and eBay sales.

Another individual had a passion for the outdoors, so he turned his hunting and fishing hobbies into opportunities to network with those who had similar passions, thereby making himself one of the most successful Hummer salespeople in the country. (And, in an adaptive selling approach characteristic of the highly passionate, he has proactively been keeping his clientele satisfied with other brands now that Hummer is defunct.)

Yet another top performer found a way to satisfy his deepest passion through his work: "I'm a spiritual guy. I believe in serving other people. That's all we do—we're just servants. If I serve you the way you want to be served, you're going to be so excited about that. I don't even have to ask you to buy a car from me. I don't have to ask you to send me a referral."

The notion of finding an environment to fit one's preexisting interests and mindsets is both very old and very new. Consider an 1890 corporate newsletter of the Singer Manufacturing Company, a sales powerhouse of its day, that contained the following aphorism: "If the salesman cannot bring himself to believe in himself, his house, and his goods, he is either very badly placed, or he has mistaken his calling." Identifying a job that fits well with your skills and further molding the job environment to strengthen that fit still works today. We—the authors of this book—have different passions: writing, speaking, the intellectual challenge of complex research, selling new projects, building the business, and so on. We work together at the same company, but we have found ways to structure our individual jobs so that we can focus primarily on our individual passions. It isn't always easy, and sometimes it requires restructuring our workdays, our staff, and our division of labor among ourselves. But we persist in finding ways to strengthen the fit of job and skill, as that has proven to be the key to both professional success and personal happiness.

Most sales training efforts have been unsuccessful because they have focused on molding the individual to fit the system. Certainly some of that needs to be done; salespeople must understand the product line, communicate their brands in a consistent manner, understand the corporate culture, and so on. But ultimately it's about finding what interests you and then choosing or molding environments appropriately. Done with too much drive, it can be off-putting. Excessively molding (some might say manipulating) one's work environment can come across as overly self-serving and be perceived as disrespectful of the corporate culture and one's coworkers. That's precisely the complaint one colleague had about Ross Perot: "The problem I had with Perot is that if the game doesn't go the way Ross wants it to go, he keeps trying to change the rules so that he wins." But ultimately, taking charge of their environment, and bending it to their needs, is one way that highly successful people come to thrive.

University of Montreal psychology professor Geneviève Mageau summed up her research on the topic this way: "Passion comes from a special fit between an activity and a person. . . . You can't force that fit; it has to be found."[25] One of her studies found, for example, that kids were more likely to develop a passion for music if they were given the autonomy to structure how they would approach music—choose their instruments, their genre, their practice schedule. Interestingly, although some kids in less self-chosen environments became passionate about music, they were more at risk for showing an unhealthy obsession rather than a productive and thriving passion.

* * *

The take-away: Sales managers must rethink their roles in a discover-your-passion-and-mold-your-environment world. Their job becomes less about managing and more about unleashing. It's less about enforcing rules and more about helping people creatively bend them. This is particularly true because many salespeople are attracted to the field in large part for the autonomy it provides.

The Labels and Expressions of Passion

The label itself doesn't particularly matter: positive thinking, optimism, engagement, leveraging strengths. We use the word *passion*. These are all expressions of the same underlying phenomenon. And let's be clear: We're not advocating an effortless "get passionate and success will come" philosophy. Passionate people achieve more because they think differently, they act differently, and they even feel differently from the rest (see Table 2.4).

TABLE 2.4

Behavioral, Cognitive, and Affective Manifestations of Passion

	Passion is characterized by . . .	Passion is *not* characterized by . . .
Behavioral	• Approach • Activity • Pro-activity • Engagement • Focus • Effort and motivation • Follow-through • Effective use of time • Learning and reading • Networking	• Avoidance • Inactivity • Reactivity • Procrastination • Distraction • Avoidance
Cognitive	• Positive thinking • Optimism • Internal locus of control • Self-efficacy • Perceived mastery	• Pessimism • Learned helplessness • Rationalization
Affective	• Positivity • Happiness	• Fear (of rejection, failure) • Withdrawal • Burnout

Source: Harrison Group.

Passionate People Are Magnetic

Passion is easily apparent. Everyone can literally see it—quickly. Harvard psychologist Nalini Ambady found that a 30-second video clip of sales managers discussing their work is enough for people to accurately distinguish the top sales managers from the average ones.[26] In fact, people do even better at this task if the verbal content of their statements is filtered out, allowing observers to ascertain only body language and tone of voice. Actually listening to what the people say, it turns out, gets in the way. Dr. Ambady and her team suggested that observers are picking up on strong interpersonal skills, and they assume those skills lead to enhanced job performance. That certainly plays a role, but we believe that observers are also picking up on the sales managers' passion for their work and for life. We asked a man who had sold over $1 billion in real estate what he thought was the secret to the success of top salespeople. He responded: "It's not just about a passion for the job. It's about a passion for life. They have an energy. People want to be around them."

Passionate People Learn More Effectively

Passionate people bring a fundamentally different approach to learning, and in how they respond to challenging situations. For example, social psychologist Carol Dweck and her colleagues have shown that people with a learning orientation, which focuses on acquiring new skills and mastering new situations, tend to achieve more than people with a performance orientation, which focuses on demonstrating competence and avoiding perceptions of incompetence.[27] In other words, some people pursue things because they love them, want to learn more about them, and master them. Others are more externally motivated.

The results are clear: Salespeople with a learning orientation set more ambitious goals, work harder, plan better in approaching their sales territories, and more thoughtfully prioritize which accounts to pursue, and as a result, they outsell those with a performance orientation. And when the going gets tough (and in sales, that's a regular occurrence), the reactions of the two groups couldn't be more different. People with a learning orientation consider challenges as an opportunity to grow, to develop, to further their sense of mastery. People with a performance orientation avoid challenging situations, and when forced to confront them, they bring a "playing not to lose" approach; they prefer the certainty of an easy win, and they fear that struggling in a challenging situation will cause others to think negatively of them.

Passionate People Are Hardworking and Resilient

Passion goes hand in hand with persistence, determination, and high levels of effort. A lack of passion usually means being derailed by minor setbacks and giving up easily. It's true in life, and it's particularly true in sales, where many jobs are filled with rejection. Popular sales books are filled with inspiring anecdotes and motivational tales of great persistence. Some point to Thomas Edison, whose 1,093 patents remains a record, and they cite his famous remark that success is 1 percent inspiration and 99 percent perspiration (or, if they are more quippy, "Everything comes to him who hustles while he waits"). Others tell the story of Mark Victor Hansen and Jack Canfield, who were supposedly unable to sell their book idea to the first 123 publishers they approached. Their *Chicken Soup for the Soul* and its many sequels have since sold literally tens of millions of copies (although the story is often told with an insightful twist; they got all those rejections in a single day at a publishers conference).

The importance of passion and persistence is why many popular sales training books are equal parts sales training and motivational self-help manuals. In addition, popular self-help gurus such as Tony Robbins, Zig Ziglar, and Brian Tracy all have strong contingents of salespeople among their fans, and they all have books, audio programs, and seminars specifically targeted to salespeople. Whatever one may think of today's crop of motivational gurus, it is hard to argue with the fundamental truth that passion and persistence are crucial to success in life, as well as in sales. For example, people who successfully maintain their New Year's resolutions for at least two years report an average of fourteen slips or setbacks during that time.[28] They succeed, but only because they persist.

Passionate People Fine-Tune Their Strategies

Albert Einstein is frequently credited as defining insanity as "doing the same thing over and over again and expecting a different result." Passionate people are persistent, but they also fine-tune their strategies for pursuing their goals—in other words, they are resilient *and* flexible. This is precisely what effective salespeople do as well. In the research literature, it's called adaptive selling behavior (ASB), and it's been shown to improve sales performance in a variety of studies.[29] It requires first a recognition that different approaches are needed for different prospects. But it also requires a confidence in your ability to pull it off, which is helped by practice and experience. And it often requires additional research, in understanding both the unique interests of the prospect and the different ways you can deliver what would meet his or her needs. As always, it starts with interest and passion, but it only impacts bottom-line performance with practice and hard work. Nevertheless, it's worth the effort. So take a moment to revisit how you might be able to adjust your sales strategies in specific situations, based on what's working and what's not. For example:

- Phone calls not getting through? Try e-mail.

- The customer doesn't want à la carte pricing?
  Put him on a retainer.

- The customer isn't picking up on your usual subtle hints about when orders need to be submitted?
  Try being a little more blunt about timelines.

Passionate People Move Toward Desired Outcomes

People of passion set goals more effectively, resulting in them feeling "pulled" toward their goals as opposed to pushing themselves. Their success comes, in part, from knowing what they want to pursue, not simply what they want to avoid. Psychologically, this distinction is crucial. People who focus on moving toward desired outcomes, as opposed to setting "avoidance goals," are:[30]

- Physically and psychologically healthier

- More satisfied with their lives and their relationships

- More committed to their goals

- Less upset after setbacks, and more resilient after setbacks

- Characterized by a sense of autonomy and control over their lives

- Happier when they eventually achieve their goals

- More mentally focused on positive memories and triumphs

- Characterized by a "want" mindset, rather than a "should" mindset

Passionate People Live Better

The power of passion even goes beyond something as fundamental as goal setting. It impacts every aspect of life.[31] People with a clear, compelling, nonconflicted view of what they want in life are happier. They are more satisfied with their lives. They take action more and ruminate less. They do better in school. They achieve more in their careers. They experience less depression and anxiety. They have better physical and psychological health. They are more successful at making life changes, such as losing weight or keeping New Year's resolutions. They are characterized by a strong sense of honor, solid values, and deep integrity.

That's quite a list.

THE NEXT STEP

It should be pretty clear by now: Discover your passions. Rediscover lost ones. Pursue them. Indulge them. Follow where they lead you. If you aren't passionate about your job, then get passionate. Improve the fit, or get a new job. Seriously.

And read the next chapter, which discusses the second passion that defines successful interactions between the affluent and those who sell to them.

CHAPTER THREE

The
Passion of the
Prospect

"A man without passion is only a latent force, only a possibility, like a stone waiting for the blow from the iron to give forth sparks."
—HENRI FRÉDÉRIC AMIEL

"If I were to wish for anything, I would not wish for wealth and power, but for the passionate sense of what might be."
—SØREN KIERKEGAARD

PASSION IS MORE THAN just the defining element of top salespeople. It is also the predominant characteristic of financially successful people; in fact, for most of them, pursuing a passion other than money has been the driving force behind their financial success.

This observation may come as a surprise to some, who might be tempted to think that the highly successful are primarily motivated by money. When we began our research on the financially successful back in 2005, we also looked into how marketers and the general population felt about the affluent. We discovered that there are as many myths about the affluent as there are about salespeople. The average American, for example, views wealthy people as something akin to Mr. Burns from *The Simpsons*—old, greedy, unconstrained by any sense of morality or public good. Our study *American Attitudes Toward the Wealthy* showed that the vast majority believe the wealthy are self-indulgent, lucky, self-serving snobs (see Table 3.1).

Most people we surveyed believe that the wealthy have inherited their money, a picture reinforced not only by the Rockefeller caricatures in pop culture (including Mr. Burns and Donald Duck's miserly uncle Scrooge McDuck) but also by celebutantes such as Paris Hilton. These archetypes of American wealth get more than their share of screen time, but they aren't terribly representative of the wealthy. The lives and lifestyles of the financially successful are, in reality,

TABLE 3.1
How Americans Describe the Wealthy (% surveyed)

Living lavishly	80%
Coming from families with money	79
Being in the right place at the right time	75
Somewhat arrogant	72
Self-indulgent	71
Not understanding how it is for those who don't have money	70
Not paying enough taxes	66
Snobs	62
Self-serving	60
Lucky (don't earn it)	55
Having sacrificed their principles for money	51

Source: Harrison Group, *American Attitudes Toward the Wealthy*, 2006.

quite different. For instance, over 95 percent of the affluent and the wealthy have created their own wealth. Most created their wealth relatively recently, with the vast majority of American wealth having been created in the past two decades. And as a result, most are still learning how to deal with the pleasures and challenges of abundance.

Most of the financially successful grew up in the expanding American middle class of the 1950s, '60s, and '70s. Today, their average age is in the upper forties. They have a tremendous belief in education; over 80 percent of them are college graduates and nearly half hold advanced degrees, but they are far more likely to have attended a public college than an Ivy League one. They also believe in the importance of family; that is, they got married, had kids, and have largely been successful at keeping their families together.

They have worked hard, typically for a long time with a respectable but not spectacular salary. Financial abundance often came suddenly, in a liquidity event triggered by a company's going public or being acquired, or a bonus afforded a new partner or some other watershed business moment. On average, this liquidity event happened about ten years ago. Most of them are still learning to live with abundance, but they have held on to their middle-class attitudes; in fact, most still describe themselves as middle class at heart.

Conspicuous consumption garners the headlines, but it is as unrepresentative as are images of inherited wealth. Most of the successful live lives and buy products that are subtle and understated, a tendency that accelerated during our recent Great Recession, as phrases such as "logo shame" entered the lexicon and displays of wealth came across as insensitive rather than impressive. When it comes to brands, they look for quality, craftsmanship, and service. The social and emotional qualities of brands, such as making one feel or appear successful, are much less influential in their purchases. Table 3.2 shows the contrast between myths and realities regarding this group; Table 3.3 captures some of the group's essential beliefs and attitudes.

THE BIGGEST MYTH
ABOUT THE AFFLUENT

Perhaps the most enduring myth about the affluent is that accumulating money is their primary motivation in life, their raison d'être. Instead, they are most often people who pursued a passion. They worked hard. They typically had good timing or a bit of good luck, and often some of both. And their efforts to pursue their passion took off to a degree that almost surprised them. Financial abundance followed, but it was more as a symptom or aftereffect than the primary motivation.

TABLE 3.2
Myths and Realities of Today's Wealthy

Myth	Reality	
Inherited riches	Entrepreneurial riches	
Conspicuous consumption	Stealth wealth	
Brand as badge	Brands enable self-expression	
Trophy wife	First wife	
Ivy League	State university	
Old patriarchs	Boomers and Xers with kids	
Elitist attitudes	Middle-class attitudes	

Source: Harrison Group and American Express Publishing, *Survey of Affluence and Wealth in America*, 2010.

Key Findings	
Average % of assets from inheritance	2%
I believe in "stealth wealth"—having money, but keeping it under the radar	82
Expressing my personal style is very important to me	69
Married to first spouse	64
% of college grads attending public colleges; Ivy League	59; 14
Median age; % with kids under 18	47; 50
I would describe myself as middle class at heart	84

TABLE 3.3

The Journey of the Affluent, in Their Own Words

Middle-Class Upbringings

"I lived on Elm Street USA. . . . [Years later] I went back there, and it was like, ooh, the house wasn't as big as I thought, and, ooh, those trees just weren't as large as I thought they were. But, in my mind they were huge, and it was great, and the yard just went forever."

Risk-Taking Entrepreneurship

"My transition from the corporate work-a-day world to [running a successful business] involved first giving it all up, sacrificing, and living on a vineyard without electricity. Without running water. Without a toilet. In a double-wide mobile. With an 18-month and a 3½-year-old. With no income, no cash flow, no nothing. Nose diving into debt. All to get this thing up and running . . ."

Years of Dedication and Sacrifice

"Somehow over the years, folks have gotten the impression that Wal-Mart was something I dreamed up out of the blue as a middle-aged man, and that it was just this great idea that turned into an overnight success . . . . Like most other overnight successes, it was about 20 years in the making." —Sam Walton, founder of Wal-Mart

Caution and Stealth Wealth

"The first call I got was my brother-in-law looking for a loan. My friends thought I had changed. It's no wonder I spend much of my time disguising my success."

Maintaining Integrity and Moral Fiber

"Though I am grateful for the blessings of wealth, it hasn't changed who I am. My feet are still on the ground. I'm just wearing better shoes." —Oprah Winfrey

Managing Money Across Generations

"Our kids are great. But I would argue that when your kids have all the advantages anyway, in terms of how they grow up and the opportunities they have for education, including what they learn at home, I would say it's neither right nor rational to be flooding them with money." —Warren Buffet

Redefining Retirement

"The ability to bring on top executives for a large-sized business gives me the luxury of essentially not working. I'm kind of halfway between president and chairman. You know, I'll take the summer off and go to Europe with the kids, and it's not an unexpected thing, because I do it pretty much every summer. And there's a team there that knows how to run it, knows what level of things I need to be involved in. I've got [a colleague] coming in twice a month to kind of look things over for me, help me out. He's retired; he doesn't want to stay home all day, so it's a good thing for him, it's a good thing for me."

Source: Harrison Group and American Express Publishing, *Survey of Affluence and Wealth in America*, 2010.

In our survey of the financially successful, we asked the participants about these dynamics—about the relationships among money, striving, and success. They responded:

- "To me, money is the by-product [of] professional activity, the passion, the enthusiasm, and the knowledge of your subject. . . . The goal has never been [to make] money. The goal has been [to learn, to have] adventures, have fun, share."

- "I didn't care to get to the top. I never tried to get to the top. I tried to do a good job and they put me there in spite of it or because of it."

- "We worked real hard to build this company—my wife and family and myself. We looked around one day, and my business gave us a lot of things we never dreamed of. But it was the work, and what we were able to do for our customers and the people in this town, that made us happy. I guess I can't say that I'd be happy if we were poor, but I don't want anyone to think being able to buy what we want makes us happy. . . . [B]eing able to do what we want makes us happy."

Certainly, passion characterizes how most of these successful individuals approach their careers, although perhaps it is more precise to say that they have aligned their careers with their passions. Regardless, it was the ensuing career success that generated their income and assets. They are the entrepreneurs, the CEOs and their C-level brethren (CFOs, CPOs, COOs), the lawyers, the accountants, and other providers of professional services. As people rise out of the affluent ranks and into the more rarified air of the truly wealthy, they are mostly business founders and CEOs.

The vast majority remain on the front lines of their businesses, working well beyond meeting their financial needs, quite simply because it was never really about the money. Most of them agree that their career is a "critical element" in their self-esteem, and nearly half agree that their lives revolve around their careers. Three-fourths feel that they work harder than most people they know. And doing business in today's difficult economic climate spurs additional challenges; fully half say, "My job now requires that I work harder for less reward." In fact, when we asked for the secrets of their success, "hard work" topped the list, followed closely by "determination," "intelligence," and "education."

THE PASSION FOR FAMILY
AND THE "WE NEED" ECONOMY

Aside from their passion for their work, the other great passion in the lives of the affluent is family. Freud famously called work and love the foundations of modern human life,[1] and this certainly seems to be the case among today's affluent. Eighty-two percent of our surveyed group are married, including 64 percent who are married to their first spouse. Three-fourths describe themselves as "a much more involved parent than my own parents were with me," and a similar number eat dinner together as a family at least four nights a week. Only 19 percent feel misunderstood by their kids. Indeed, the family spirit runs strong; it even transcends the human species: Ninety-four percent of pet owners in this group consider their pets "part of the family."

Two of our wealthy research participants explained:

- "The key to success in life? [laughter] A happy family life, having a happy, positive business life, and being able really in your business to provide a service or product for your customers. And then being happy with the service that you provide for them."

- "[Success in our family life is about] sharing passion. Certainly, that's a big thing for us. Because we are both so committed to [our business], it would be very separating if only one of us was involved in that."

The Economic Downturn Strengthens the Family

The strong focus among the affluent on the family has intensified, not weakened, as a result of the economic downturn. When the going got tough, the team pulled together. Nearly 90 percent feel they have "done a good job of making my household more fiscally responsible," and two-thirds agree that "my significant other and I have learned to work together because of the economy."

This represents a fundamental shift in how consumers weigh their purchasing priorities. The early and mid-2000s were characterized by an "I want" economy: a consumer-meets-Caesar ethic of "I came, I saw, I bought." Magazines were glossy enticements to consumption, thick with ads, less focused on encouraging the urge to purchase than on channeling the presumed urge to purchase toward a particular brand. The stock market was rising; home values were strong. Seven in ten affluent individuals described themselves as extremely or very optimistic about the future. Family was important, to be sure, but consumption in the service of individual desires consumed significant emotional and financial resources.

The future seemed bright—that is, until 2006 and the crash of the subprime housing market. In truth, we began to see significant purchasing and general economic anxiety in our surveys throughout 2006. Since there were few general economic threats, other than soaring real estate debt, to justify the magnitude of anxiety we were seeing, we referred to this advancing fear as the start of the "emotional recession." That is, optimism about the future was dropping. Concerns about the long-term stability of the housing market were creeping in. The pollsters' "right track/wrong track" measures showed growing numbers of consumers as uneasy with the direction of the country.[2] America was battling international terrorism and was engaged in two expensive land wars. There was a growing sense that our society—business, government, and individuals—had simply been living unsustainably beyond its means.

Spending cutbacks accelerated throughout 2007, and the National Bureau of Economic Research (the private, non-profit group of economists charged with dating recessions) would later peg the official start of the recession at December 2007. But the emotional underpinnings were apparent over eighteen months earlier. In reality, it was 2006 that had seen the transition from an "I want" economy to an "I need" economy. Anxiety was in the air. Discretionary spending was cut to an absolute minimum. Perceived risk was ever-present. The diminishing role of consumption and acquisition was met with a sense of sadness and self-deprivation. It would only get worse.

As 2008 started, our research showed consumers cutting back even further. In September 2008, the government decided that Lehman Brothers was not too big to fail, and the company's subsequent bankruptcy sent shockwaves through the markets. The fear catapulted into a full-scale financial panic when the October 2008 financial statements were opened. Christmas 2008 was a time of change for families and merchants, as well as an inflection point for the American economy as a whole. Consumers hedged the loss of purchasing power, in part, by shifting their shopping online. At that time, many retail stock-keeping units, or SKUs, particularly those relevant to the holiday shopping experience, could be purchased online at substantial discounts from keystone retail prices. So, trapped between cutting back or moving their purchasing to the lowest cost channel, retailers were caught unprepared, and they offered huge discounts to unload inventory. Still, low prices were met with even lower consumer interest, making the holiday season of 2008 one of the worst in history.[3]

Retailers were better prepared for the 2009 holiday season, now holding less inventory and ready with value-oriented offerings, but in terms of consumer enthusiasm for spending, 2009 showed little improvement over 2008. By early 2010, optimism among the affluent had jumped significantly, but a majority of them still expected the recession to last longer than a year, and spending continued to be significantly suppressed.

Throughout this economic tumult, affluent families got tighter and stronger. Spouses talked more openly about money, and marriages held together. Parents talked about money with their kids and soothed their fears; they started spending less on their kids, and kids actually appreciated the financial responsibility that kind of restraint reflected. Money continued to be spent, for sure, but increasingly it was on things for the family. *The "we need" economy had arrived.* For example, while spending on fashion and jewelry continued to drop, spending on family vacations was one of the first categories to see an end to consumer cutbacks.

Certainly there were changes in spending patterns among the affluent. Weekend getaways were up, while multiweek vacations were down, for example. And there were changes in value expectations, too. When we asked affluent families how their personal travel plans were expected to change as a result of the recession, the most common response was that they would stay in the same quality of accommodation, but they would expect a better deal. It remained a challenging environment for travel and lodging providers at all price points, but for their customers it was clear that the desire to bring the family together was deemed a worthwhile reason for spending the money.

Lasting Changes in Spending Patterns

Not only has the passion for family pulled the affluent closer during these challenging times, but our research has shown that it has even reshaped the process by which household decisions get made. Certainly most big decisions are team decisions, but it is most often the female head of household who is the team leader. She is, within the typical American family (affluent and otherwise), effectively the chief executive officer, chief financial officer, chief purchasing officer, and chief operating officer. We've called this paradigm shift the "New American Matriarchy," or more informally, the "mom-ocracy." Our research has shown that she is more likely than the male head of household to be responsible for most household tasks, ranging from scheduling household appointments and making most purchases, to paying the bills and making investment decisions.

A majority of affluent women agree with the statement, "In the end, my opinion determines the family financial decision." In fact, the only household task that men are more likely to be responsible for is mowing the lawn. Move over, glass ceiling, the grass ceiling is here. Her shopping style tends to be thoughtful and precise; the result is a growth in affluent shopping patterns that are so savvy and sophisticated that they are reminiscent of how businesses make purchasing decisions. Mom makes decisions through discussion and consensus, not by fiat. Everybody's opinion is solicited and considered, including the kids'.

MONEY, CULTURE, AND THE NICHE PASSIONS

If career and family are the top two passions for the affluent and wealthy, what other factors come into play? The answer is that there is no clear third-place winner. From there, our research shows that the passions of the affluent are highly idiosyncratic. What excites one person inspires yawns from another. Travel comes closest—a passion for half of our respondents. Foodies, wine buffs, and music lovers are overlapping categories of passion, but each accounts for about one-third of the surveyed population on its own. Certainly the affluent like money, as virtually everyone does, and we've seen that money is not the primary motivation in their career strivings. Only 29 percent describe themselves as passionate about money, making them about as prevalent among the wealthy as are book collectors, techno geeks, political junkies, shopaholics, health fanatics, and the sincerely religious (see Table 3.4).

TABLE 3.4

What the Affluent Are Passionate About
(% surveyed; top 20 interests shown)

	Total
1. Family	64%
2. Travel	52
3. Music	35
4. Fine cuisine	31
5. Wine	31
6. Books/Rare books	29
7. Money	29
8. Technology	26
9. Politics	24

10. Shopping	23
11. Health and Beauty	22
12. Religion/Faith	22
13. Theatre/The arts	21
14. Science	20
15. Cars	18
16. Charity	17
17. Architecture/Interior design	16
18. Art	16
19. Fashion	16
20. Fine watches and jewelry	14

Source: Harrison Group and American Express Publishing, *Survey of Affluence and Wealth in America*, 2010.

Notable by their absence from Table 3.4 are what one might characterize as "the Robin Leach passions"—the yachts, champagne, exotic cars, cigars, and other accoutrements of opulence so prominently featured on *Lifestyles of the Rich and Famous*, or its more recent progeny, *Cribs*, or in the music videos that exemplify the aspirations of a new generation. In fact, these interests are found among only 5 to 10 percent of the affluent population (see Table 3.5). Of course, these are not insubstantial numbers in absolute terms; that is, the 10 percent of the affluent who are passionate about exotic cars, for example, constitutes a market of roughly 1 million people. Still, these aren't the passions of the majority.

TABLE 3.5
Niche Passions of the Affluent
(% of those surveyed)

% Passionate About . . .	Total
Exotic/vintage cars	10%
Champagne	9
Yachts/Boats	9
Cigars	5
Thoroughbred horses	4

Source: Harrison Group and American Express Publishing, *Survey of Affluence and Wealth in America*, 2010.

But even among those who are passionate about a niche category, money often remains a barrier to full-bore consumptive participation, as a connoisseur or as a collector. Consider that 5 percent of the affluent are passionate about cigars, and 4 percent describe themselves as cigar connoisseurs or collectors. Put another way, with few barriers to entry, 80 percent of those with a cigar interest follow through with significant spending. In contrast, less than half of those who are passionate about a niche interest such as exotic cars or yachts actually "convert" to being collectors (see Table 3.6). Still, connoisseurship remains a collection of niches—no single realm captures more than 20 percent of the market.

The same pattern emerges from a study of the philanthropic efforts of the affluent (see Table 3.7). Eighty-six percent agree with the statement, "I am passionate about the causes I give to," but no single type of charity predominates. In fact, the growing trend is for the affluent to start their own foundations, to ensure that their money and their efforts go precisely to their areas of interest.

THE ARC OF MATURATION AND THE EVOLUTION OF PASSIONS

Living with abundance is a learning process, a journey for which the affluent's middle-class backgrounds did not prepare the members of this group. Generations of Rockefellers,

TABLE 3.6

Percentage of Affluent Who Are Collectors/Connoisseurs
(% of those surveyed)

	Total
None of these	53%
1. Wines/Champagne	19
2. Fine cuisine	14
3. Books/Rare books	10
4. Antiques	9
5. Fine art	9
6. Theatre/The arts	9
7. Beer/Microbrews	8

8.	Distilled spirits	8
9.	Fine watches and jewelry	8
10.	Design (e.g., furniture, architecture)	7
11.	Fashion	6
12.	Cigars	4
13.	Vintage cars	3
14.	Exotic cars	3
15.	Vintage watches/Jewelry	3
16.	Yachts/Boats	2

Source: Harrison Group and American Express Publishing, *Survey of Affluence and Wealth in America*, 2010.

TABLE 3.7

**Percentage of Affluent Who Contribute to
Specific Charity Types (annual % for those surveyed)**

Church/Religious organization	46%
Health/Medical	39
Local community cause	39
Child/Children-specific	37
Education	33
Homeless/Poor	33
Animal-related	26
Political	19
Environmental	18
International relief organizations	17

Source: Harrison Group and American Express Publishing, *Survey of Affluence
and Wealth in America*, 2010.

Carnegies, and Mellons learned from the collective wisdom of their families about sophisticated spending, investment, and philanthropy. They grew up hearing about the subtleties of buying at the high end in literally hundreds of categories. They experienced the sublime distinctions of quality, materials, and heritage that separate Chanel from Coach, Armani from Aeropostale, Rolex from Timex, Ritz Carlton from Radisson, Tiffany from Zales, first class from coach.

Today's wealthy have to figure it out for themselves. Over 80 percent of the affluent describe having money as "a real learning process." Most of them have been hit up for money by family or friends. Half of them have been, in their words, "ripped off." They learned the good and the bad, mostly by themselves, mostly on the fly, as one explained:

> *"My husband and I are the first generation to enjoy the wealth that we have created, so there are lots of surprises along the way—things you don't expect. And there's nobody putting their arm around you helping you figure things out. . . . For instance, when we took the company public, nobody said: 'Here are five things that you need to really think about.' There were a lot of things that I was absolutely blindsided by. There is an incredible learning curve."*

Those living with affluence for five years or less—a segment we call "Apprentices"—are characterized by lingering feelings of unreality and a pervasive sense of caution. A majority worry about running out of money. Memories of leaner times are fresh in their minds. Many have had sudden changes of fortune for the better, but they remain anxious that their situations could reverse themselves just as quickly. They have seen their social standing change, again, for better and for worse. They find themselves in exciting but unfamiliar new social circles, while feeling that many old relationships are strained. They fear money will change them and erode the work ethic of their children. They shop cautiously, avoid the highest-end products, and are wary of status symbols. In short, *Apprentices are reluctant to embrace new passions, for fear of losing touch with their middle-class sense of self, and they are cautious in indulging their current passions.*

Over time, Apprentices mature into "Journeymen." Time—and in many cases, multiple liquidity events—have begun to assuage their fears. As they reach a comfort zone and are content with acquisition and consumption, they begin to dabble in luxury products in categories to which they have always been drawn. They experiment in indulging their passions. They buy their first seriously expensive toys. And upon seeing the expensive toys and objets d'art of their newly made wealthy friends, they characteristically ask, "Where did you get that?" Existing passions evolve, broaden, and deepen. They grow over time, with experience, with connections to those who share similar passions. And with greater exposure, any modest interest may evolve into a true passion, particularly when cost barriers are eliminated by growing wealth. *Consider that Apprentices, on average, have three passions, but during the Journeymen phase, the affluent typically acquire at least one or more new passions.*

After fifteen years of living with abundance, the wealthy evolve into "Masters." Typically their wealth has snowballed. Many have joined the $1 million/$10 million club: $1 million in income and $10 million in assets. They have become comfortable with wealth and the lifestyle it affords. They have, or are working toward, a thought-out and systematic approach to the "big picture" issues of wealth: business succession, estate management, and charity. They maintain many of their middle-class attitudes, particularly in the emphasis on quality and value, but they bring a worldly sophistication and appreciation for subtlety that has been honed for years. They spend more. On everything. Whether it's homes or fashion or technology, their reluctance to pull the trigger on spending is gone. *Masters indulge their passions without hesitation, and they enter the small world where the movers and shakers in their areas of interest all seem to know one another.*

Some passions are the "you-have-them-or-you-don't" variety, consistent in their prevalence across the arc of maturation: family, music, wine, food, books, shopping, health, religiosity, science, charity, and fashion. In these areas, Apprentices and Masters are equally likely to express an enthusiasm. Other areas of passion show distinct growth; with more time and money, and with greater experience in the joys of a category, their interests evolve into passions. Examples of these include travel, art, theater, design, cars, and politics. When we switch from looking at the "merely" passionate to those who describe themselves as connoisseurs and collectors, the growth across the arc of maturation is evident in virtually every area—microbrews and spirits are the only exceptions (see Table 3.8).

101

TABLE 3.8

Affluent Who Are Collectors/Connoisseurs (% of surveyed)

	Total	
None of these	53%	
1. Wines/Champagne	19	
2. Fine cuisine	14	
3. Books/Rare books	10	
4. Antiques	9	
5. Fine Art	9	
6. Theatre/The arts	9	
7. Beer/Microbrews	8	
8. Distilled spirits	8	

Tenure with Wealth		
Apprentices <5 yrs	**Journeymen 6–14 yrs**	**Masters 15 yrs+**
60%	52%	48%
15	20	22
12	12	19
8	12	10
5	9	12
4	8	15
6	8	13
9	9	7
8	6	9

(continued)

TABLE 3.8
(continued)

	Total	
9. Fine watches and jewelry	8%	
10. Design (e.g., furniture, architecture)	7	
11. Fashion	6	
12. Cigars	4	
13. Vintage cars	3	
14. Exotic cars	3	
15. Vintage watches/Jewelry	3	
16. Yachts/Boats	2	

Source: Harrison Group and American Express Publishing, *Survey of Affluence and Wealth in America*, 2010.

Tenure with Wealth		
Apprentices **<5 yrs**	**Journeymen** **6–14 yrs**	**Masters** **15 yrs+**
7%	9%	9%
4	7	11
3	4	10
3	3	5
3	2	5
2	2	5
2	3	4
2	2	4

THE ARC OF MATURATION AND
SELLING FINANCIAL SERVICES

The arc of maturation is, ultimately, a process of learning about the power of money. So perhaps it comes as little surprise that the members of these three segments—Apprentices, Journeymen, and Masters—approach investing and financial services very differently. Apprentices, as we have seen, are risk averse. They fear running out of money, are accumulation-focused, and shy away from complex financial instruments. Journeymen are financially aggressive, and they introduce significant diversity into their portfolios. Masters like to think of themselves as very conservative, focused on long-term (often multigenerational) planning for their wealth, but they pursue it in a way that would be objectively characterized as aggressive (e.g., extending into hedge funds, commercial real estate, private equity funds, even thoroughbred horses). Figure 3.1 summarizes the financial perspectives of the three segments.

The key to success for those selling financial services becomes identifying where a prospect is in the arc of maturation, and tailoring the sales approach and portfolio recommendations accordingly (recall our discussion of "adaptive selling behavior" in Chapter 2). Obviously, coming straight out and asking, "So how long have you been rich?" will raise a red flag, so a more subtle approach to gathering information is required, usually by listening intently to any information offered proactively or easily elicited.

FIGURE 3.1
Financial Concerns Across the Arc of Maturation

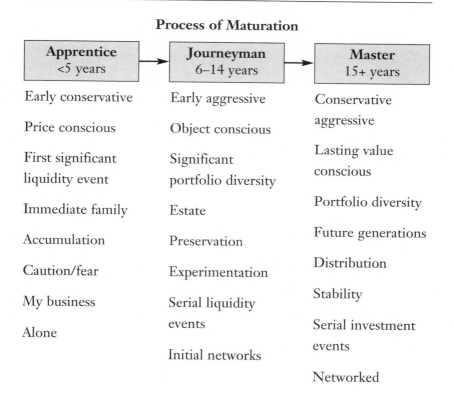

Process of Maturation

Apprentice <5 years	Journeyman 6–14 years	Master 15+ years
Early conservative	Early aggressive	Conservative aggressive
Price conscious	Object conscious	Lasting value conscious
First significant liquidity event	Significant portfolio diversity	Portfolio diversity
Immediate family	Estate	Future generations
Accumulation	Preservation	Distribution
Caution/fear	Experimentation	Stability
My business	Serial liquidity events	Serial investment events
Alone	Initial networks	Networked

At the risk of overgeneralization, we give you some indications of status. You are talking with Apprentices if:

- They agonize over risk.

- They fear making mistakes.

- They ask you what you do.

You know you are talking to Journeymen when:

- They talk about what other people think of them.
- They ask you where you got something.
- They want to be given inside opportunities.

And you know you are talking to Masters when:

- They have an informed view of risk.
- They have reserve cash for passions such as collecting and giving.
- They ask you about your family.

Now that you have identified a prospect and his or her likely needs, the next step is to tailor your approach. Table 3.9 lists some do's and don'ts for each segment.

PASSION AS THE MISSING INGREDIENT IN SALES

We've shown passion as the defining element in the lives of both top salespeople and the wealthy prospects to whom they sell. Here's the disconnect: Most wealthy people believe salespeople lack passion. In our *Affluent Attitudes Toward Salespeople* survey, we asked people to estimate what per-

TABLE 3.9

Do's and Don'ts of Selling to Wealthy Segments

Embracing Apprentices	
Do	**Don't**
Educate systematically	Try to end-run their instincts
Introduce to planning	Sell what they don't understand
Accept material goals	Surprise call
Offer to help the kids	Tell them jokes
Advance charity	Understate risk
Help with cash management	Talk about other people
Talk about the journey	Fail to listen
Ask about their business	Insist on a level of risk
Describe your role	Clean out their cash
Check back often	Talk "inside"
Keep it simple	Insult their intelligence
	Be impolite
	Compete by insult

(continued)

TABLE 3.9
(continued)

Embracing Journeymen	
Do	**Don't**
Educate on risk	Fail to communicate (at least monthly)
Offer new ideas	
Introduce estate planning	Forget their family
Introduce managed accounts	Forget their charity
Entertain	Forget their names
Call on ideas	Forget to instruct
Encourage liquidity planning	Be afraid to tell the truth
Introduce team	Be unkind
Set up kid's accounts	Become pushy

Embracing Masters	
Do	**Don't**
Schedule account reviews	Be their friend
Family wealth planning	Be uncomfortable with their other advisers
Estate updating	
Offer complex investments	Fail to be punctual
Offer venture investments	Make promises you can't keep
Offer private placements	Delegate without permission
Distribution planning	Let your staff treat the client with disdain
Listen and think	
Offer resources	Fail to be accountable
Advise	Forget cash
Go 24/7 anywhere in the world	
Be careful with risk	

centage of salespeople in a given category they have experienced as truly passionate about their jobs. Purveyors of art garnered the highest ratings: two-thirds of them are believed to be passionate about their work. The best that the other ten categories can muster is a figure hovering near the Mendoza line of 50 percent, as shown in Table 3.10. In high-end financial services, jewelry, real estate, and luxury retail stores, affluent consumers believe their odds are only 50-50 of working with someone who truly cares. Clothing boutiques and upscale department stores fared even worse, and only one in four expects it from used-car salespeople.

SUMMING UP

The previous chapter explored the role of passion in sales success; as a result, we suggested renewing and intensifying your efforts to discover and deepen your passions. This chapter painted a detailed portrait of today's affluent, rich with implications for sales success. To sell to the affluent, you address middle-class sensibilities and speak to today's understated preferences. You also sell to the family as a team, with the female head of household as leader. You express your integrity and maintain and communicate your quality. Table 3.11 pairs these sales qualities with the values of the affluent and wealthy.

TABLE 3.10

Fields in Which the Affluent Perceive Salespeople as Passionate (% surveyed)

Art	68%
New luxury automobiles	51
High-end financial services	49
Jewelry	48
Real estate	48
Home and entertainment technology	46
Branded stores (Chanel, Louis Vuitton, Gucci, etc.)	45
Clothing boutiques	41
Home furniture & décor	38
Upscale department stores	38
Pre-owned automobiles	26

Source: Harrison Group, *Affluent Attitudes Toward Salespeople*, 2010.

TABLE 3.11
Summary of Key Take-Aways

The Affluent and Wealthy ...	Successful Salespeople ...
1. Worked hard to pursue a passion	Understand, and connect with, the passions of their prospects
2. Have middle-class backgrounds and mindsets	Sell to the middle-class sensibilities of today's affluent, not stereotypes of celebutantes or aging patriarchs
3. Are still learning to live with abundance	Help them become sophisticated about the category
4. Believe in stealth wealth	Help customers "defend" their purchase as practical, prudent
5. Care deeply about integrity	Have integrity. Take pride in the brand's integrity. Communicate it.

6. Make decisions as a team	Sell to each member of the team, and facilitate its collaborative decision making
7. Are worried about running out of money	Recognize that price concerns are psychological barriers as much as economic barriers
8. Take pride in being resourceful	Realize that resourcefulness makes the customers feel smarter, not deprived; reinforce this new pride
9. Have not lowered their brand standards	Realize that resourcefulness and value orientation don't mean a willingness to trade down in quality or amenities
10. Are getting happier	Facilitate happiness; be happy

THE NEXT STEP

The biggest implication of this information is that successful salespeople need to understand the passions that inspire their prospects. Take a "passion census" of your customers. Do you really understand their businesses? Their families? Their hobbies and interests? In sales training seminars, we often ask salespeople to write a "personal ad" describing their target in detail. Then we ask them to list the in-person or online communities ("watering holes") that might attract their ideal prospect. For example, in Chapter 2 we mentioned that we worked with one of the top Hummer salespeople in the country, and he identified a passion he shared with most of his prospects—a love of the outdoors. He then joined several groups focusing on hunting, fishing, conservation, and other topics of interest among those who shared that passion. Lo and behold, he found himself surrounded by like-minded individuals who happened to be ideal prospects for the Hummers. And as GM wound down the Hummer brand, he was able to transition into selling brands that still spoke to the passion he shared with his customer base.

CHAPTER FOUR

The
Passion of the
Product

"Pleasure in the job puts perfection in the work."
—**ARISTOTLE**

THE THIRD ELEMENT in successful interactions between salespeople and their affluent prospects is a passion that is evident in the product or service being sold. Indeed, that's the very essence of luxury.

There is a point in the range of every product category where the merely excellent is surpassed by the truly exquisite. Luxury products and services are those that offer consumers *sublime* quality, performance, and emotional connections. In this sense, passion and luxury have intertwined DNA. Both are fundamentally about *going beyond*. Both are about transcending the utilitarian, the merely necessary, the simple must-have.

Consider the utilitarian object made unique by passion-spurred artistic expression, whose flourishes may seem superfluous to the untrained eye but are rich in meaning, beauty, and symbolism to those in the know. Or observe the passion evident in engineering excellence that far exceeds the practical tolerances needed under the most demanding of conditions—the automobile capable of going faster than the driver will ever go and cornering with g-forces that exceed human tolerance. Or the watch whose precision is measured atomically in microseconds—slices of time far thinner than human beings can discern.

Sometimes exquisite excellence can be remarkably easy to appreciate. Not simple to make, or simple to do, but rather simple to recognize and comprehend. Great beauty can be very accessible, immediately engaging the human visual and aural instinct for excellence:

- You don't need to have seen a thousand royal tiaras to see one at Cartier and instantly understand why the French jeweler has been called "Jeweller to Kings, King of Jewellers." The unique designs and exceptional quality of gemstones from Tiffany's are obvious the first time you see them.

- The brilliance and genius in the music of Mozart, Gershwin, and McCartney was recognized immediately, each in his own time. There was a simplicity and earnestness to the guitar playing of Eric Clapton that led his early followers to paint "Clapton is God" graffiti around London, anticipating what would become a legendary career. You probably knew there was something extraordinary about Led Zeppelin's classic "Stairway to Heaven" the first time you heard it.

- If you play golf at, say, Pebble Beach, you can appreciate the excellence of the course even if you haven't seen a golf course before. You will know from the color of the greens, the sharpness of demarcation between fairway and rough, the beauty of the landscaping, the contrast between the cypress trees and the grass, the meeting of earth, sea, and sky. There's a simplicity to this elegance, a tastefulness and clean beauty that strike an emotional chord even among the uninitiated.

The message of this chapter: *Those with a passion for the product study the passion of the product.*

DISCOVERING THE ESSENCE OF LUXURY

Despite the examples just given, and many others like them, quite often what constitutes a luxury product, and hence what is the manifestation of passion in that product, is less accessible. The essence of luxury is not always obvious to the uninitiated; its recognition and enjoyment require education and experience.

For example, most people can't tell the difference between a $20 supermarket bottle of wine and a $10,000 bottle of Domaine de la Romanée-Conti. Then again, most people, even many with otherwise sophisticated tastes, don't care. Most are happy to have an experience good enough to satisfy their modest interests and typical tastes. Among those who do care are those who struggle to discern the subtleties of varietal, vintage, and vineyard. *But those with a passion for the product also study, and come to appreciate, the passion that went into making the product and that is manifested in the product.*

The wine enthusiast aspires to, and appreciates, the sublime experience that wine critic Clive Coates articulated so eloquently when he called the Domaine de la Romanée-Conti Pinot Noir "the purest, most aristocratic and most intense example of Pinot Noir you could possibly imagine. Not only nectar: a yardstick with which to judge all other Burgundies."[1] And these enthusiasts have personally experienced the disappointment sometimes felt by those early in the learning curve, as when travel writer Bruce Palling concluded: "But like many of life's most trumped up experiences, DRC vintages are not always so thrilling on first encounter."[2]

Those with a passion for the brand feel emotionally connected to all the expressions of passion in that brand—its heritage and values, its strengths and styles. For example, DRC enthusiasts learn:

- The history of the tiny slice of France's Burgundy region that is Domaine Romanée-Conti, from the ancient Romans who tilled the land two millennia ago, to the Benedictine monks who lived there one millennium ago, to its being named *Romanée* for reasons unknown in 1631

- That the area was purchased in 1760 by the Prince de Conti, Louis François Ier de Bourbon, after he outbid his nemesis, Madame de Pompadour, mistress of France's Louis XV

- That the land was seized and sold during the French Revolution, only to fall into the hands of Napoleon's henchmen

- The modern history as well, including how horses have replaced tractors (to minimize soil compaction) and how biodynamic principles have become central to the DRC philosophy

- That the tremendous scarcity of its wines is not a calculated marketing ploy but a result of a tiny vineyard's producing wine that typically is aged two to three decades or more before reaching maturity

The affluent whose passion is DRC wines embrace its full history, and the deep thoughtfulness of those who continue that history today—what you could term the passion of the product.

THE FIVE DIMENSIONS OF TRANSCENDENCE

Passion and luxury are intertwined concepts and these concepts share the phenomenon of multifaceted transcendence. In great brands, this transcendence typically occurs in terms of their *history, scarcity, craftsmanship, clientele,* and *materials.* Choose a luxury brand that has stood the test of generations, such as the DRC wines, and the dimensions become readily apparent. As other examples, let's consider the following three case studies.

Louis Vuitton

In 1835, a humble young Louis Vuitton (the man, before there was a brand) traveled by foot from his home in the Jura region of France, bordering Switzerland, taking odd jobs along the way to finance his 250-mile journey. It took him *two years.* His journey was at a time when people in Western Europe had a case of wanderlust. The industrial revolution had produced rapid growth in steamship travel, as well as expansion of railroads and paved streets. The newly wealthy from this manufacturing boom were developing a passion for travel and their need for well-made luggage was growing.

Passions intertwined. Vuitton worked an apprenticeship for the master Malletier Monsieur Marechal and was soon creating the finest luggage available for the wealthy and royalty. But his style and sensibility was honed by true excellence in craftsmanship. His details were not superficial flourishes but, rather, hallmarks of excellence in design that a true traveling aficionado would appreciate. For example, most of the luggage of the time used a traditional rounded top. Vuitton noted that this made them hard to stack, so he introduced innovations such as lids that are lightweight, airtight, and flat. These innovations became part of his signature style—an approach that began with, but eventually transcended, utilitarian need. Competitors copied his design, so he innovated again, introducing unique canvas patterns, logos, and even trademark statements that extended his signature look and further reinforced the brand.

Louis Vuitton died in 1892, but under his son George's leadership the company embarked on what we would today call a series of brand extensions. Such changes can often have a diluting effect on a brand, but Louis Vuitton navigated this path with products that built on their core offerings and saw no diminution in quality or aesthetic standards. For example:

- "Steamer bags" were expensive but popular accessories for keeping dirty clothes inside LV trunks.

- "Keepall bags" were light travel bags that offered an easy alternative to heavy trunks for shorter getaways.

- "Noe" was introduced in the 1930s, a champagne bottle carrier for the supposedly strong market of Parisians seeking to transport several bottles at once. Instead, the Noe's elegance and limited occasions for use led women to use it as a handbag, and thus the LV handbag juggernaut was born.

In 1936, George Vuitton passed away and ownership of the company was transferred to his son, Gaston-Louis Vuitton. New products, including purses, wallets, and bags, and the now-classic cylindrical "Papillion" bag, were launched. Instead of making compromises and stagnating, the company produced aesthetic innovations with new canvas and utilitarian advances with new leather coatings that added strength and durability without compromising quiet elegance.

Today, Louis Vuitton headlines LVMH, one of the world's largest luxury goods conglomerates (home to brands such as Dom Pérignon, Fendi, Marc Jacobs, TAG Heuer, Sephora, and Donna Karan). But Louis Vuitton has maintained everything that made the brand great: uncompromising quality materials, superlative craftsmanship, and strong ties to its history of passion. The innovation continues in its award-winning and buzz-inducing advertising campaigns, featuring celebrities as diverse and distinctive as singer Jennifer Lopez, actress Scarlett Johansson, Soviet ex-leader Mikhail Gorbachev, and Rolling Stones guitarist Keith Richards. The strength of the brand has served the company remarkably well, and it has been managed with remarkably apt stewardship.

When the breathtakingly bad holiday season of 2008 saw many luxury brands discounting by 50 percent or more, Louis Vuitton held the line on prices, communicating its brand strengths and value proposition; the company came through in much better shape than many of its competitors. Thus, the five dimensions of transcendence—history, scarcity, craftsmanship, clientele, and materials—are the connecting threads that run through the story of Louis Vuitton and still drive the financial performance of the brand today.

Chanel

Before Gabrielle Bonheur "Coco" Chanel revolutionized fashion with her little black dress, bobbed hair, sling pumps, and cardigans, her early life was characterized by poverty and tragedy. Her father was a market stallholder, and her mother a laundrywoman; when she was twelve, her mother died of tuberculosis and her father abandoned the family. Coco spent six years in an orphanage, where she learned to sew. She left the orphanage at age eighteen, and after an unsuccessful stint as a cabaret singer, she discovered the world of elite Parisian fashion. Her passion was less for the clothing itself and more for finding sartorial and artistic expressions of her beliefs and values. She was giving women a wardrobe that was simultaneously elegant and professional, which both was distinctly feminine and nevertheless sent a clear message of "hands off, buddy." Simply put, her passions were at the intersection of beauty and empowerment. Indeed, she delighted in having her styles copied and made accessible at low cost to millions of women around the world.

With the guidance of wealthy sponsors, she was able to set up her shop in 1910 with several hats and "one dress, but a tasteful dress." Within a few years, Maison Chanel was a fashion house to be reckoned with. Tremendous innovations followed, driven by her vision and passions. She introduced the tricot sailor frock and the pullover sweater; she unearthed wool jersey from its longtime service as underwear fabric and put it to use in soft, clinging dresses. She created the first ever designer fragrance sold. She ushered in gypsy skirts, embroidered silk blouses, and accompanying shawls. Her quality standards were exceptional—the stitching invariably perfect, the designs without flaw. She would say, "The essence of luxury lies not in the ornateness, but in the lack of vulgarity."

Chanel remains a remarkable company today. Coco Chanel never married and never had kids. But her spirit, her breakout personality, and the vocabulary of competence that she introduced to women's fashion still infect the spirit of the place. Her life was uniquely her own. She smoked. She spoke her mind. She sang in cabarets. Her multimillion-dollar jewelry collection was built largely with the help of wealthy male suitors. When the Duke of Westminster proposed marriage, she turned him down, saying, "There are a lot of duchesses, but only one Coco Chanel." She dressed Ingrid Bergman and Marlene Dietrich, Princess Grace and Queen Fabiola, the Rothschilds and the Rockefellers.

The French avant-garde artist Jean Cocteau would later say, "If Mademoiselle Chanel has reigned over fashion, it is not because she cut women's hair, married silk and wool, put pearls on sweaters, avoided poetic labels on her perfumes, lowered the waistline or raised the waistline, and obliged women to follow her directives; it is because—outside of this gracious and robust dictatorship—there is nothing in her era that she has missed."[3] Hers was a life lived with passion, indeed. Those passions continue to run throughout the company and products that still bear her name.

Hermès

Consider the passion in the company that Thierry Hermès founded under his name in 1837. His uncompromising approach to excellence in materials and craftsmanship won him the business of making harnesses and bridles for royalty. He won the First Class Medal of the 1855 Exposition in Paris, and in 1867, the Exposition Universelle. In 1880, the second generation of the Hermès family built a shop at 24 rue Faubourg Saint-Honoré and added saddlery to their product line. They acquired the rights to using a zipper, opening the door to expand from leather goods to handbags and clothing. In 1935, the company introduced its famous "Kelly bag." Named after the actress who married royalty, the beautiful Grace Kelly, this bag paved the way for the handbags that Hermès is perhaps best known for today.

We reviewed the exceptional materials and craftsmanship (not to mention the authentic scarcity) behind Hermès handbags in our earlier book, *The New Elite*, but those passions extend throughout its product line, including ready-to-wear fashion, perfume, watches, gloves, tableware, soaps, and ties. Consider the iconic Hermès scarf; the details of design and manufacturing are unique and exquisite. Hermès starts with the finest raw Chinese silk, which is woven into a yarn stronger and heavier (and therefore longer lasting) than that used in most other scarves. The hems are hand stitched to exacting standards. Designs are printed onto the scarves by hand, not by machine (videos of this process are available on YouTube). The printing is done one color at a time, with a waiting period of up to a month while one color is allowed to dry before another is added. It takes literally hundreds of hours to make an Hermès scarf, resulting in an authentic scarcity. The designs themselves are truly works of art. *The Hermès Scarf: History & Mystique* is a 300-page coffee table book that celebrates the 2,000+ scarf designs Hermès has created since the product's first introduction in 1937. As with Hermès handbags, the clientele for these scarves is memorable, including Audrey Hepburn; Catherine Deneuve; Jacqueline Bouvier Onassis; Hillary Clinton; Sarah Jessica Parker; Queen Elizabeth II (who was depicted wearing one on a British postage stamp); and, of course, Grace Kelly (who once famously used an Hermès scarf as a sling after injuring her arm). In recent years, new designers have been brought in for fresh takes on this classic, but what they produce always is true to the spirit and the passions of the original brand.

Like Louis Vuitton, the company has a strict policy about not discounting its prices—a policy that has served the company well during the challenges of the Great Recession. And its policy of destroying (not discounting) unsold merchandise has helped protect the value of all its brands. In every respect, from manufacturing and marketing to service and sales, Hermès strives to remain uncompromising and transcendent.

Thus, Hermès is a brand that prides itself on exceptional materials and impeccable craftsmanship. People are willing to wait for several years to get their hands on one of its creations.

THE TOPOGRAPHY OF EXCELLENCE

Great salespeople understand the brands they represent. They can give detailed descriptions of the brand's history and heritage. They can tell stories of how generations of management have stayed true to the values and ideals of the founder. They can relate tales of excellence in materials and craftsmanship. Yes, of course, they know their brands. But beyond knowing their own brands, they *understand the rules and standards of sublime excellence in their category.*

Consider how this understanding plays out in a curious phenomenon among luxury brands. Among the affluent, there is, in fact, surprisingly little loyalty to luxury brands. To continue our Hermès example, most women who own Hermès bags love them. But liking the Hermès brand is different from being loyal to the brand. The fact is that most women who own a Hermès bag also own a Louis Vuitton bag. And a Prada bag. And a Fendi bag. And maybe a couple of Coach bags that they bought when they began experimenting with luxury brands in that category, and that they still use on occasion. In fact, women who purchase high-end handbags own an average of more than two dozen such handbags, reflecting a variety of brands.

Handbag enthusiasts aren't typically loyal to a particular brand, but they are loyal to excellent handbags. They pay close attention to the standards of true excellence that separate luxury, quality handbags from their mainstream counterparts. And they make purchase decisions based on those criteria more than on brands per se. Consider that each year approximately 15 percent of affluent women buy a handbag priced at $500 or more. Remarkably, this number has remained unchanged even through the Great Recession. That 15 percent of women are passionate about the category, and though we were in a recession, affluent people continued to buy in their categories of passion. They showed very little interest in trading down in quality, though they have certainly been willing to trade down in quantity. That is, they are buying one Birkin bag a year instead of the three they bought in 2005. But those who are passionate about the category are confident in the ability of Hermès (or Gucci, etc.) to continue to create handbags to those standards. They also realize that others can deliver to those standards, and therefore the ability of any brand to deliver can falter.

In addition to understanding their brands, successful salespeople understand their competitors. Suppose you are selling Steuben glass, and you often tell the detail-rich stories that communicate the transcendence of that brand. But it is just as important you know that your main competitors are probably Limoges and Baccarat, and that each can deliver on excellence in the category, though they have very different stories.

Baccarat, for instance, sells products with a sparseness of design, an abstract sensibility; often the form is highly stylized and the details are absent. Limoges offers an abstract design with a lot of detail (in the eyes and ears of an animal, for example), but there are color flourishes as well. Steuben makes something polished and finished, replete with contrasts to create prismatic radiance (allowing the walls to light up with rainbows when the sun hits it). A real collector typically owns all three and knows why. And glories in the differences and the similarities among them.

Again, brand loyalty takes on a different meaning in the luxury field, and salespeople must be prepared to help their prospects navigate the full breadth of offerings.

REPORTS OF LUXURY'S DEATH ARE GREATLY EXAGGERATED

It should come as no surprise that the second half of the 2000s was a challenging time for luxury providers. But in many respects, in many markets and in many categories, luxury is surviving and even thriving. In fact, it could be said that the passion market has been the one market that hasn't collapsed. Yes, real estate prices fell precipitously around the country. But in any major metropolitan area, the neighborhoods characterized by true quality and authentic scarcity held their value. In San Francisco, it is Sea Cliff and Pacific Heights. In Dallas, it is Highland Park. In Chicago, it is Lake Forest. In Los Angeles, it is Beverly Hills and Brentwood. In Houston, it is River Oaks.[4] And so on. For the most part, high-end vacation homes of exceptional quality have held their value better than midmarket time-shares. Diamond prices have fallen throughout the recession, with the exception of truly flawless large stones, for which prices have grown.[5] In fine art, it is the works by the Old Masters and modern and contemporary artists with established reputations that have held their value; works by lesser known artists and new works have fallen in price (leading some to say that "the mediocre never sells except to the naïve"). In all of these examples, the products are bought to satisfy the buyer's passion, and they are owned for their steady or increasing value. But the best assurance of value at purchase is the multifaceted transcendence that feeds the affluent person's expression of passion.

Fortunately for luxury marketers, there is life in the luxury marketplace as a whole, and not just at the very highest end. Our research has shown that, as of mid-2010, three key indices of luxury spending are trending up (see Figure 4.1). They are still short of pre-recession levels, to be sure, but there are encouraging signs:

FIGURE 4.1
Luxury Interest Indicators, 2008–2010

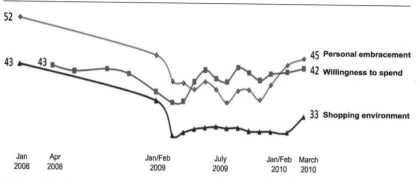

Source: Harrison Group and American Express Publishing, *Survey of Affluence and Wealth in America*, 2010.

- *A Willingness to Spend.* There is not just the raw willingness to open one's wallet but also attitudes such as, "I think a few luxuries are important in tough times."

- *A Shopping Environment.* There is a modestly growing desire for elegant and interesting in-store luxury retail experiences.

- *An Embracing of Brand Identification.* A growing number of people believe that "the brands I wear say a lot about who I am," and "I kind of like it when others recognize me as being wealthy." The luxury guilt and logo shame that characterized 2008 and 2009 has diminished significantly.

THE NEXT STEP

Redouble your efforts to be a student of what you sell. Be a student of your category, your industry, and your competitors. Understand the expressions of excellence and passion in them.

Tell stories like those we told about Louis Vuitton, Hermès, and Chanel. Or whatever the equivalent might be for you. Real estate agents, for example, should know the details of craftsmanship and construction that speak to quality and express a passion for building. They should know when a home was built, by whom, and for whom. They should be historians of the cities and neighborhoods in which they sell, and knowledgeable about changing architectural styles. They should be guides to passion.

CHAPTER FIVE

Theory into Practice: Thirteen Expressions of Passion in Selling

"An ounce of action is worth a ton of theory."
—**RALPH WALDO EMERSON**

*"In theory there is no difference between
theory and practice. In practice there is.*"
—**YOGI BERRA**

AS MENTIONED IN CHAPTER 1, the most successful interactions between salespeople and their affluent prospects bring all three passions together:

- A salesperson with a sincere love for what he or she does

- A prospect who is pursuing a sincere interest

- A product with transcendent properties

Two people arrive, of their own free will, in an environment of their mutual choosing. The shared interests are apparent. Rapport is established quickly and easily. The meeting of minds in terms of needs and wants is of primary importance; price considerations are secondary, at best. The transaction satisfies and furthers the interests of all parties—buyer, seller, and manufacturer.

The three passions do not always come together so effortlessly, however. This chapter explores thirteen straightforward, authentic ways to leverage the passions inherent in a sales situation. For each, there are exercises that will help you put these ideas into action and help close sales.

1. Express the love of your job.

2. Tell detail-rich stories.

3. Discover a shared pursuit.

4. Give the docent's tour.

5. Understand their ultimate passion: family.

6. Satisfy the passion du jour: value.

7. Use the language of passion.

8. Understand that reliability is "the new trust."

9. Create a ritual of celebration.

10. Communicate a compelling brand promise.

11. Hone a compelling elevator pitch.

12. Ask passion-based questions.

13. Sell to happiness.

EXPRESSION 1:
EXPRESS THE LOVE OF YOUR JOB

"When any fit of gloominess, or perversion of mind, lays hold upon you, make it a rule not to publish it by complaints."
—SAMUEL JOHNSON

"Choose a job you love and you will never have to work a day in your life."
—CONFUCIUS

Of the hundreds of ways for a salesperson to turn off a prospect, perhaps the easiest is simply this: to complain. About anything. Your job, your hours, your commission—or lack thereof. The bureaucracy that holds you back. The boss who doesn't appreciate or understand you. The seemingly endless recession. The product or service you sell can be a source of so many complaints, but the most common one is usually that it costs too much: "If only the powers that be would lower the price, I could sell the crap out of X."

No job is perfect. No day is without disappointment or distraction. It's normal to feel frustration. It's just not wise to express that frustration to your customers. Samuel Johnson, quoted above on the wisdom of withholding complaints, concluded: "The usual fortune of complaint is to excite contempt more than pity." He was right. Prospects have their own problems. They are working with you to help solve those problems. Or prevent them. Or, at the very least, put them out of their minds for a little bit while they focus on something more pleasant. Prospects aren't there to hear about your problems. In fact, what they really want to hear is just the opposite. They want to hear about how much you love your job. As one of our wealthy research participants put it:

> "For me, the ideal salesperson is somebody who loves their job. I want to make their day happy, and I want them to make my day happy. You can usually see it and feel it, right away, when somebody really loves what they're doing. . . . When I sense that, I'll spend! I will. I just want to say to them: 'I'm so happy that you're happy!' I'm going to come back and I'm going to use that salesperson again and again and again."

Our research has shown, and our sales training work has confirmed, that simply declaring a love and an enthusiasm for your job can be a powerful rapport builder. Indeed, one of our training programs suggested that this technique alone could generate as much as a 20 percent increase in average revenue per customer.

The psychological dynamics behind this simple technique are surprisingly complex. The fact is that the class differences between a member of the financial elite and the typical salesperson are fully apparent to both, and it can be cause for discomfort for both. The customer typically believes in stealth wealth, not simply to avoid being targeted but also because it is authentically consistent with the values of modesty and humility so prominent in their middle-class upbringing. They recognize that this salesperson is likely "not of the class," and this hampers the customer's willingness to disclose both his or her purchasing motivations and a personal evaluation of the product or service at hand.

You, as salesperson, can imagine how a customer who fears being judged as shallow, wasteful, and pretentious might be hesitant to say something like, "I'd like to get a Cartier Pasha watch to replace the Bulgari Diagono watch I lost while sailing in the Caribbean. I'd like to pay around $5,000, but I don't want it to look too blingy—know what I mean?" On the other side, as salesperson, you can also feel uncomfortable, particularly if you are relatively new to working with the wealthy. This can be an intimidating, nerve-racking experience. You're apt to fear coming across as not sufficiently knowledgeable about the products, and/or unable to understand the needs and lifestyles of the wealthy customer.

Expressing your love of your job can be a potent way for you to ease that unspoken and potentially disruptive class divide. As we have seen, in most cases today's wealthy individuals did not set out to accumulate tremendous wealth. Instead, most are entrepreneurs and business executives who pursued a passion, and wealth was an almost accidental side effect of their hard work and eventual success. By expressing a love of your job, you make both you and the customer feel more comfortable. It creates a powerful shared connection: The customer is no longer a wealthy prospect and you are no longer an intimidated salesperson; you are two individuals who pursue their passions.

Here's an important caveat: *Expressing your love of your job must be sincere.* Any lack of authenticity will be patently obvious. Today's financially successful have fine-tuned their BS detectors. Successful entrepreneurs and senior executives have heard many sales pitches; indeed, part of their professional success has come from their ability to size up situations, to evaluate sincerity, and to gauge the ability of someone to deliver on promises.

EXERCISES

List five things you love about:

- Your job

- Your customers

- The products or services you sell

Practice telling stories that:

- Demonstrate your passion for your work

- Describe your most satisfying interactions with customers

- Illustrate your sincere interest in the products or services you sell

EXPRESSION 2:
TELL DETAIL-RICH STORIES

"It's the little details that are vital.
Little things make big things happen."
—JOHN WOODEN

"Storytelling is an ancient and honorable act.
An essential role to play in the community or tribe."
—RUSSELL BANKS

These days, talk is cheap. Sales pitches are easily discounted and routinely dismissed. Today's sales environment is fraught with distrust. Persuasion through advertising has become tremendously challenging, and the medium itself has largely come to focus on simply building awareness as a result.

The question becomes: How do you enhance believability in an environment of distrust? Product demonstrations can play a role, as can testimonials. But in selling to the affluent, perhaps the most powerful verbal tool in the salesperson's arsenal is telling a great story, rich in detail.

We've all heard the saying "The devil is in the details," and we can appreciate its message that the execution of lofty plans is more challenging than the creation of those plans. But perhaps even more telling is the quote upon which the German proverb is believed to be based, generally attributed to French novelist Gustave Flaubert: "The good God is in the detail." On the whole, we're inclined to side with Flaubert. Details are extremely powerful, almost transcendent.

Chapter 4 explored many examples of how sublime details are what separate true luxury products from their mainstream competitors. Details of history and provenance. Details of exquisitely sourced and mixed materials. Details of engineering and craftsmanship. Of clientele and of meaning.

Here we discuss the power of details, which is twofold. First, details make stories engaging, a fact that writers over the centuries have understood well. As Vladimir Nabokov counseled, "Caress the detail, the divine detail." Details engage attention, arouse the senses, and inflame the emotions, for good and ill; as English novelist Ruth Rendell put it, "The knives of jealousy are honed on details." Details cut through the attention filters that people put up to deal with the barrage of advertising images and sales pitches that bombard them. They perk up. They tune in. They start listening more intently, and that's precisely what you, as a salesperson, need.

Second, details not only engage the attention, they also inherently make a story more believable and make the salesperson who provides them more credible. In contrast, descriptive terms and vague adjectives—like *luxurious* or *prestigious*—gloss over details and hide a lack of specific knowledge.

Consider two hypothetical salespeople for the Italian firearms company Beretta. Salesperson A, who lacks detailed knowledge about the company and its products and uses vague descriptions to cover up that lack of knowledge, explains that Beretta is an Italian company with a long history of making excellent firearms for buyers around the world. Salesperson B, in contrast, explains that Beretta is actually the oldest corporation in the world, with its first transaction taking place in Venice in 1526. Today, after nearly 500 years, Beretta is still run by a direct descendent of the founder, and it is recognized as the finest manufacturer of firearms in the world, with customers including the U.S. Army, the Marine Corps, and police departments around the world.

Think about the tremendous differences in these few simple sentences from two different salespeople. Salesperson B gave us a considerably richer story. Venice, not Italy. The "oldest corporation in the world" founded in 1526, not simply a "long history." Their customers include the U.S. Army and Marine Corps, not just "buyers around the world." Excellence is not simply stated but is implicit in details, such as 500 years of nearly continuous management by a single family and its reputation as the finest manufacturer of firearms in the world. Which story grabs your attention?

Which one convinces you of the salesperson's superior product knowledge? From which salesperson are you more likely to buy? Details provide the proof points, demonstrating both the quality of the brand and the quality of the salesperson.

E X E R C I S E

Craft and practice detail-rich stories about:

- The origin and founders of the company you represent

- The history of the brands you offer

- The provenance of specific products and offerings

- How high-end offerings in your category differ from mainstream offerings

- Spectacular, mutually rewarding customer service (preferably by you)

- Tremendous customer loyalty

- How your company treats customers and employees extremely well

- How working for your company is different from working at other jobs

---

EXPRESSION 3:
DISCOVER A SHARED PURSUIT

"Shared joys make a friend, not shared sufferings."
—Friedrich Nietzsche

In Chapter 2, we explored the long history of marginally successful research on top sales performers. It's worth revisiting one of those less than dramatic predictors: the similarity between the salesperson and the prospect. In the 1960s, it was a topic of considerable research. Similarity on dimensions as mundane as age, height, product preferences, ethnicity, and even smoking were mildly associated with greater rapport and stronger sales.

There's no denying the phenomenon: People like to work with people similar to themselves. It's just that there's a limit to it. No matter how much emotional comfort is provided by similarities, prospects won't buy from a salesperson who doesn't know what he is doing, or if the value proposition isn't right, or for any of dozens of other reasons. Yet, there's no denying the connection and rapport-building power of discovered similarities.

Much of the research from the 1960s focused on similarities along demographic dimensions. Today, we would argue (and hope) that demographics and personal characteristics hold much less sway than they did five decades ago, particularly in a society where most women work outside the home and most people have equal civil rights under the law. Perhaps our assumptions about modern society are overly optimistic, but it's been our experience that dimensions of similarity today are far more impactful if they are chosen, rather than innate, characteristics. *Ultimately, it's a shared passion or shared pursuit that brings the greatest bond.*

The question then becomes how to uncover the pursuits and passions of your customers and prospects. We explored this question earlier in the book but offer another tool here: modest self-disclosure. Relationships are ultimately about reciprocity: responding to a question with an answer, asking a follow-up question to show your interest in understanding the person better, returning a phone call, returning a favor, and so on. If at any time the dance of reciprocity stops, the relationship falters. A modest self-disclosure is a gambit in the game of reciprocity, a subtle expression of your interests that begs for a similar disclosure in return. You might disclose your hobby, your weekend plans, your favorite movie, a cute story about your kids, your most recent purchase in the category—whatever might catch the prospect's attention and potentially deepen the conversation about what you're selling. As one top performer told us:

> *"I have a view of the selling process as involving a great deal of reciprocity. The object is for them to buy something from me, and for me not to buy something from them. And the question is always: How do you balance their rather overloaded contribution to my rather underloaded contribution? Some*

salespeople do this with lunches. Some do it with all kinds of little acts of entertainment. In the world of reciprocity, the fulcrum balances on reciprocal disclosures of intimacy. So the client is going to have some disclosures about money that I won't have to make. I am really willing to tell stories that make myself look fumbling, or share some personal information that might be tangentially related to the sale, to try to put people at ease. . . . It's not that I'll say anything, but I'll say what needs to be said to communicate to the client that I'm approachable and I have something in common with them."

EXERCISES

- Observe your customers closely to better discern what their interests might be. Notice what they wear, what's in their offices, what they drive, what appointments they have before or after meeting with you, the stories they tell about their family, and so on.

- Make a modest self-disclosure and observe whether it is reciprocated and ultimately deepens the relationship.

EXPRESSION 4:
GIVE THE DOCENT'S TOUR

"[From] the Latin word docēre, *meaning 'to teach'. . .
Docents are educators, trained to further the public's
understanding of [an institution's] cultural and historical
collections. . . . They are normally volunteers . . . [who]
undergo an intensive training process . . . which teaches
them good communicative and interpretive skills, as well
as introduces them to the institution's collection and its
historical significance. They are also provided with reading
lists. . . . Docents are kept up-to-date with continuous
training and seminars. Docents can be found at many
institutions, including local and national museums, zoos,
historical landmarks, and parks."*
—WEBSTER'S ONLINE DICTIONARY

When it comes to selling luxury, those who do it best are
equal parts salesperson and museum docent. Consider the
parallels. The fine art in a museum, for example, needs
explanation and education for most people to fully understand and appreciate it. To untrained eyes, a Rembrandt
looks a lot like a Renoir and a Picasso a lot like a Pollock.
Into the educational void steps the docent, who must:

• Know history in order to place the artist in historical
  context; to understand the social movements and other
  artists he or she was influenced by (or rebelling against);
  to fit the work into its social context.

- Understand the provenance and history of specific works of art, supplying stories of past owners and past exhibitions that engage attention and perhaps provide some mystery (e.g., "The *Mona Lisa* was owned by both Louis XIV and Napoleon before being moved to the Louvre, where it was stolen in 1911. . . ").

- Be able to communicate the subtle differences that distinguish one artist from another, or an artist's early efforts from his or her late works.

- Know the materials and processes in detail—drawings or paintings, oil or watercolor, canvas or paper, representational or abstract.

- Answer questions "off the top of his or her head" and without condescension. In a docent's museum or a salesperson's showroom, a response of "I'll find the answer and get back to you" doesn't meet customer expectations.

In short, docents are masters at educating people on subtle points of differentiation, and, in particular, the details that separate the merely good from true masterworks. And in one of the ultimate displays of passion for a topic, they do it for free. Few patrons hesitate to interact with them ("Hey, they're passionate about the topic—of course they'd like to talk with me and answer my questions"), and few question the objectivity of their information ("It's not like they're trying to sell anything . . ."). In terms of storytelling approach and knowledge of details, most salespeople would be wise to follow the path of the docent. And although you're not expected to do your job for free, you do need to become thought of as an objective source of advice—a resource for education—and not be viewed as "selling every minute." There's another parallel between a museum docent and an effective salesperson: role of guide. A docent guides visitors through the museum, taking in the different galleries, explaining the museum's history and layout, occasionally introducing experts on this artist or that piece of work. A docent provides a mental map for patrons, one that covers the entire museum, and not just the docent's specific area of interest. A good salesperson will do the same, when possible. One top sales associate at an elite department store described her job as "not just helping customers buy from the floor I happen to find them on . . . it's a total walk."

That phrase "total walk" came up in our interviews several times. It means guiding customers throughout different departments, to different floors, exploring different merchandise. It may start with the suit, but soon extends to building an ensemble—the handbag, the accessories, the shoes, and so on. It obviously increases the revenue from that customer, but it also is more likely to turn a onetime customer into a devoted fan. The interdepartmental tour also builds a mental map for the customers, building their confidence to return to the store and navigate its many departments on their own.

We saw the docent's tour, with an interesting interpersonal twist, at one of the most successful automobile dealerships in the country. They call it a "quick tour," and it does indeed involve giving a tour of the dealership, but in a subtle and unstated way. Here's an example: Before taking a prospect for a test-drive, the salesperson makes a photocopy of the prospect's driver's license. But instead of heading into the back room to make a photocopy himself (or herself), the salesperson says: "Hey, I need to make a copy of your driver's license—want to walk with me?" And on the way there, they meet Joe, the finance guy. Joe smiles and waves; he and the prospect shake hands and exchange a few brief pleasantries. The salesperson and prospect move on, make the photocopy, and head out for the test-drive.

Toward the end of the test-drive, the salesperson asks: "Can I show you something you won't see anyplace else?" It's hard to say no to that one, and the salesperson instructs the prospect to turn into the dealership's service center. And it is, indeed, like a service center the prospect won't see anywhere else. It is spotless. Not just the waiting room, but also the service bays. For a place where cars are repaired, there is a truly remarkable lack of dirt, grease, or oil. Next to it is a warehouse of inventoried parts, equally spotless, that ensures that customers won't be inconvenienced or be forced to drive loaner vehicles while "waiting for parts to come in." The place hums with activity but isn't frenetic. The staff is busy, but calm and friendly. One gets the sense of well-oiled machines, both literally in the machinery in the place and figuratively in the systems that coordinate the people. In short, everything the prospect sees here exudes pride, preparation, and professionalism. The prospect doesn't hear about these qualities in a sales pitch but sees it for himself.

The prospect sees more unusual sights. Outside the service center cars are lined up for free car washes, which this dealership offers for life. Those washing the cars greet their customers with a smile and know their customers by name. Susan, the head of the service department, then greets the customers, again offering a handshake and quick exchange of pleasantries. Then it's back to the dealership to debrief the customer about the test-drive and listen intently to what he might want next.

Consider the power of this simple technique. The prospect has seen the entire dealership; with a mental map of the setup, the process arouses no barriers or objections. Unlike asking, "Can I show you around the dealership?" or some other question guaranteed to raise flags and slow the process, the salesperson has asked only for a walk-along to the copy machine and the innocuous question, "Can I show you something you won't see anyplace else?" Furthermore, the quick tour has subtly shown off the dealership's strengths and differentiators—with a world-class service department, it's no surprise that was a prime stop on the tour. It also has the simultaneous benefit of putting the prospect at ease socially. When it comes time to finance the vehicle, there's no fear of an ominous "finance department," staffed by unknown people who might make the process difficult. No, they are going back to work with Joe, whom they have already met, and who seemed like a perfectly fine fellow. This dealership prides itself on taking care of its customers, and also in being a pleasant place to work as well as to buy a vehicle. It's one thing for a salesperson to say it; in fact, probably every salesperson does say it. But the quick tour illustrates the proof points—everyone the customer meets seems professional and quite happy to be working there.

EXERCISES

- Visit your local museum. First, walk around for an hour, gleaning whatever insights you can, based on your own observations. Then take a docent's tour. Observe the docent's style and see how much more you learned on a guided tour.

- Revisit how you sell. How would a museum docent present—in an objective, engaging, story-based way—what you sell? What are the detail-rich stories of history and quality that are "must tell"?

- Design a docent's tour that subtly shows off the very best of the brand you offer.

EXPRESSION 5:
UNDERSTAND THEIR ULTIMATE PASSION:
FAMILY

*"A family is a place where minds come
in contact with one another."*
—BUDDHA

We saw in Chapter 3 that family interests consistently top the lists of passions for the affluent. Depending on your product category and your sales style, understanding customers' family situations may be a powerful way of deepening your relationship with those customers and prospects. But as it is the ultimate passion for these people, tread carefully on the subject of family. It is easy to invade a customer's comfort zone when it comes to sharing information about family.

Understanding the family situation is obviously of particular importance for those in sales in the financial services industry. Has a new baby changed the customer's need for life insurance? Are there more kids on the way? Has there been a financial switch from a dual-income household to a single-income breadwinner-homemaker household? Is there a child heading to college soon, necessitating that some cash be freed up for tuition payments? Is there a "boomerang kid"—one who has returned home after college, and may need some guidance in getting a job and becoming financially independent? Is an aging parent putting a near-term financial burden on your customer, a burden that may soon paradoxically morph into a significant inheritance?

It is one thing to know the ages of your prospects and their family members, and to understand the likely changes in lifestyle and income. But there's another level of understanding: knowing the needs and attitudes of family members, their personalities and preferences, their ambitions and fears. For the wealthy, for example, there is significant concern that money might undermine the tight family life they have tried to create. Among 700,000 or so households with $500,000 or more in annual discretionary income, a group that averages over $12 million in assets, fully half express serious concerns about their children's work ethic because they have grown up with money. Abundance creates new fears and new expectations. More than two-thirds of these adults want their heirs to be "stewards of the family wealth," managing it and passing it on to future generations. In contrast, only 49 percent agree with the statement: "I do not care what my heirs do with the family wealth; I just want them to be happy."

The wealthy reach out to their kids with guidance and information, particularly since the Great Recession has elevated everyone's financial stress. Three-fourths of them have taken specific steps to educate their kids about financial decision making (but most stop short of revealing the full value of their estate). Other families have chosen to "outsource" the solution; instead of dealing with it "in-house," they defer to a new cottage industry offering financial how-to seminars for children of the newly wealthy. Either way, financial service providers are obviously well advised to be part of the family education process; they just have to understand the familial "lay of the land" to position themselves effectively.

One might expect that social media sites are great places to keep up with customers and their family members, and although there is potential there, tread carefully: In general, social networking sites such as Facebook aren't great places for selling. At least for the moment, the closest technological analogy to Facebook is the telephone. Consumers love it as a medium to communicate with friends and family but find it terribly intrusive when used for marketing. Less than one in three affluent Facebook users is a friend or fan of a company or product, and less than 5 percent have made a purchase decision largely based on information and ideas found on Facebook.

Of course, the relative noncommercial focus of social media sites may change as they evolve, and they certainly evolve rapidly. But today, a number of top sales performers tell us they use social media sites less as tools for broadcasting their offerings and more for listening to their customers. They maintain a minimal presence, careful to avoid being too "salesy" or posting something they wouldn't want a prospect to know about them. Their posts tend to focus on their personal and professional passions. (For example, one salesman focuses his posts on his training for an upcoming marathon, implicitly illustrating his energy as well as his ability to set and achieve big goals.)

Instead, top-performing salespeople tend to use social media sites more for "listening" than for promoting themselves or explicitly selling. And they find that information about their customers shows up on social networking sites long before it would typically filter to their financial adviser, real estate agent, travel agent, personal shopper, personal trainer, or any number of other service providers and salespeople. Facebook isn't just about keeping up with friends and family (or playing Farmville). It's often the first venue for the dissemination of information about new jobs, new kids, new business ventures, job promotions, which kids are attending new schools, family travel plans, and so on. In short, these sites are a valuable line of communication, although that communication is surprisingly more one-sided than social media are typically thought to be.

Of course, understanding the family dynamics of a customer doesn't just help the provider of financial services. Top salespeople in many categories keep detailed customer files and use them to mark occasions (such as by sending handwritten birthday cards) important to the customer and his or her family. Ultimately, the details of gathering and using information are less important than is expressing a sincere interest in those closest to your customers.

EXERCISES

- Conduct a "family census," putting into writing everything you know about your customers' families.

- Form an action plan for learning more about your customers and their families.

- Customize your approaches and offerings to these customers. How can you meet the needs of family as well as the individual?

EXPRESSION 6:
SATISFY THE PASSION DU JOUR: VALUE

"Price is what you pay. Value is what you get."
—WARREN BUFFETT

Family has been, and will continue to be, the ultimate passion for most people. But the newest and most pressing passion—one that extends through every financial strata—is value.

Among the affluent and wealthy, we first saw the seeds of this tremendous focus on value germinate in 2006. The National Bureau of Economic Research, the private group of economists charged with dating recessions, put the start of our recent Great Recession at December 2007. In fact, we saw an "emotional recession," with declining optimism, spending cutbacks, and a growing focus on value, take root as much as eighteen months earlier. The turmoil and uncertainty of the ensuing years only served to heighten this value orientation, and it required considerable experience to navigate the marketplace with a fundamentally different set of trade-offs.

According to our survey, among the affluent:

- 86 percent prefer to shop in stores with reputations for great pricing.

- 74 percent usually wait for something to go on sale before buying it.

- 64 percent shop regularly with coupons (that's right, *coupons*).

It is important to recognize that the dynamic at work here is value orientation, not necessarily price sensitivity. In fact, across a variety of product categories, the affluent have shown tremendous reluctance to buy the lowest-cost option or to trade down in quality. When we asked how the economy was reshaping their personal travel plans, for example, one of the most common responses was: "Staying in the same quality of accommodations, but expecting a better deal." Similarly, they told us they were making fewer high-end purchases, but ones that were more personally meaningful—again speaking to the unwillingness to trade down. Nowhere is this dynamic better reflected than at Costco, which is extremely popular among the wealthy, with its unique treasure-hunt approach to a surprising range of products across price ranges. (Costco is among the world's largest retailers of high-end wines and high-quality diamonds, for example.) Wal-Mart, however, with its low-cost/low-quality approach, garners much less enthusiasm (and share of wallet) among the financial elite.

We saw similar dynamics when we asked affluent individuals what words they would use to describe themselves, and what words make them more or less interested in various marketplace offerings. The list of top ten words that describe themselves (see Table 5.1) can be summarized as wise and nearly puritanical, while the bottom ten words largely reflect the superfluous and insubstantial kind of characterization they disdain. The picture becomes even more telling when one examines the words that engage their interest in products and services: *value, values, savings, deals,* and *best.* They reflect a value orientation, to be sure, but just as important is being consistent with their values and maintaining high quality. The words that turn them off reflect those things that seem gimmicky and don't stand the test of time.

The importance of value to this group is apparent, not just in their retail choices but across virtually every other category of goods and services. Consider travel. Just a few years ago, very high-priced destination clubs and other vacation concepts were successful products among the wealthy, largely

TABLE 5.1

Words That Resonate (or Not) with the Affluent

Words That Describe Me	
Top 10	**Bottom 10**
Honest	Gambler
Reliable	Socialite
Intelligent	Cheap
Loyal	Luxurious
Knowledgeable	Trend-setter
Self-sufficient	Risk taker
Consistent	Fashionable
Family-focused	Religious
Resourceful	Worrier
Friendly	Simple

Words That Make Me More Intrested in Products/Services	
Top 5	**Bottom 5**
Value	Fab
Values	Chic
Savings	Trendy
Deals	Hot
Best	Luxe

Source: Harrison Group and American Express Publishing, *Survey of Affluence and Wealth in America*, 2010.

through a "lifestyle sell": high-end accommodations, multiple destinations, fabulous vacation experiences. Some commanded initiation fees in the hundreds of thousands of dollars, with annual maintenance fees in the tens of thousands. These clubs typically offered little in the way of equity or investment potential, but customer interest was nevertheless reasonably strong. The recession put a sudden and dramatic end to that entire business model, however. By mid-2010, interest in vacations was rising, especially a growing interest in high-quality vacation homes, fractional properties, and time-shares. Whereas in 2006, these consumers wanted a fabulous vacation experience, by 2010 they were insisting on an *investment-grade* fabulous vacation experience. And their standards for what constituted "fabulous" were no less demanding. Investment-grade quality (figuratively speaking) and value continue to be the new "must-haves," regardless of whether the offering is mainstream or luxury.

EXERCISES

- Strengthen your value equation. In workshops where we ask salespeople to list how many ways they and their brands add value, the best come up with dozens of ways.

- Revisit how you communicate your value proposition.

- Increase value instead of lowering prices.

Remember: Lowering prices is a strategy fraught with peril in luxury categories. It diminishes perceived quality, dilutes one's brand image, and makes past customers feel their full-price purchases were bad decisions. Plus, you'll find it much harder to raise prices again later—today's discounted price is tomorrow's expected price.

EXPRESSION 7:
USE THE LANGUAGE OF PASSION

"The language of truth is simple."
—EURIPIDES

"Think like a wise man but communicate in the language of the people."
—WILLIAM BUTLER YEATS

In our interviews with the affluent and wealthy, we were struck by the characteristic ways they express themselves. We analyzed these interviews and discovered that certain words and phrases were used with great regularity, and we noticed that other words and phrases were conspicuous by their absence (see Table 5.2). The words these groups use might be characterized as "the language of passion": *mission, guts, future, vision, entrepreneur, right, wrong, happy*. Generally, they express their thoughts with a clear preference for short, simple words; active verbs; straightforward nouns; and results-oriented terminology.

TABLE 5.2
Words of Character and Complexity

Embrace the Language of Character			
(Words the affluent use frequently)			
Guts	Power	Small	Alive
System	Safe	First	Open
Team	Right	Sharp	Entrepreneur
Grow	Quick	Future	Owns
Plan	Shrink	Return	Trust
Honest	Smart	Wrong	Know
Happy	Tech	Direct	Mission
New	Need	Kind	Complete
Strong	Create	Danger	Rival
Make	Fun	Awake	Beat
Passion	Drive	Vision	

In contrast, our research showed that they tend to be turned off by flowery language, anything that conveys faux sophistication, and an abundance of adjectives and adverbs. In other words, they dislike the kind of language that untrained salespeople routinely use to try to impress the wealthy. Their feeble communication strategies—both written and verbal—backfire, triggering the fine-tuned BS detectors of today's wealthy. Advertising copy for luxury products is often an example of this offense—filled with multisyllabic descriptors that obscure the message.

Avoid the Language of Complexity
(Words that marketers use, but that don't resonate)

Brilliant	Philosophical	Strategy	Wealth
Correctness	Nouveau	Overture	Optimize
Optional	Enthusiasm	Bandeau	Status
Process	World-Class	Sophistication	Sharing
Creativity	Involving	Facilitate	Politics
Envy	Rich	Candid	Categorical
Evangelize	Seamless	Bling	Luxurious
Privilege	Arabesque	Prestige	Complexity
Truthful	Entitlement	Edwardian	Lavaliere

EXERCISE

Conduct a language audit of how you communicate with prospects. Evaluate the words you use in your elevator pitch, in your sales scripts, on your Web site, in your sales collateral, and in every other aspect of your sales and marketing mix. Are you using the simplest and most powerful detail-rich language that will engage your customers and prospects?

EXPRESSION 8:
UNDERSTAND THAT RELIABILITY
IS "THE NEW TRUST"

"Confidence, like the soul, never returns
whence it has once departed."
—PUBLILIUS SYRUS

For reasons we have already explored, trust has become difficult, if not impossible, to achieve in a typical sales context. But trust is an important and multifaceted concept, and it bears deeper examination. Giving up on it completely would be premature.

Academic researchers, for example, have empirically distinguished between affective and cognitive forms of trust. In sales, *affective* trust refers to an emotional connection, a comfort level, a feeling that the provider has the customer's best interests at heart. *Cognitive trust* is a bit "colder" and refers to the rational knowledge of the provider's track record, the belief that he or she is a qualified and knowledgeable individual, the fact base that he or she has about the company he or she represents, and so on. Today, affective trust has become particularly rare and challenging for the salesperson to gain or maintain. Cognitive, rational trust may still be within reach, even though it is qualitatively different from how most people conceptualize trust.

The best approach to building cognitive trust with your prospects is to simply *do what you say you will do*. In a very real sense, reliability is the new trust. More than ever, you will be judged by your ability to execute, to follow through, to simply keep your word. If you say you will follow up with a phone call tomorrow, do it. If you say you will send a packet of information next week, do it. If you say you will publish your newsletter every two weeks, do it. If you say you will show up at noon tomorrow, you'd better do it, as one exceptional salesperson found out the hard way:

> *"Not being on time is deadly. I had a meeting at which I was selling a very complicated set of studies, with many millions of dollars on the table, to a large client in the entertainment business. I was in Century City that morning interviewing a job candidate, and I got too engaged and lost track of time. We left Century City too late to make it to the meeting unless there was perfect traffic, and of course there wasn't. I called his VP to tell him we would be a few minutes late. But we ended up being more than a few minutes late. When we arrived, his secretary came to the lobby and told me: 'He'd wait fifteen minutes for Jack Nicholson but not for an [expletive] like you.' End of deal."*

There's a deeply unfair but nevertheless real asymmetry to reliability: Keeping your word may not get you a lot of credit, but failure to do so will irreparably undermine your credibility. (Interestingly, it's much the same dynamic for environmentally friendly offerings: Being green won't get you the sale, but *not* being green may prevent you from getting the sale.)

EXPRESSION 9:
CREATE A RITUAL OF CELEBRATION

Closing a sale is cause for celebration. The salesperson's reasons for wanting to celebrate are obvious. But commemorations of a transaction are perhaps even more important for the customer. Rituals of celebration put an emotional exclamation point on an otherwise rational and behavioral event. They reduce postpurchase regret and buyer's remorse. They offer another point of connection between salesperson and customer, deepening the relationship and increasing the likelihood of the individual's becoming a repeat purchaser and a long-term customer.

Don't be put off by the term *ritual*. The event can be extraordinarily simple. Consider Hermès. Sales associates don't slap your purchase in a bag and hand it across the counter casually. It is carefully wrapped in a signature orange bag. The sales associate typically comes out from behind the counter. He or she presents it to you respectfully, with both hands, and expresses happiness for your purchase. As rituals go, it's fast, simple, and powerful. Years ago, Saturn leveraged the emotional power of a ritual of celebration as well.

In a classic ad, it showed sales associates gathered around to celebrate a customer's purchase of her first car. They gave her the keys, everyone applauded, and the emotional impact was immense.

> ### EXERCISE
>
> Create a ritual of celebration to mark the "consummation" of transactions with your customers.

EXPRESSION 10:
COMMUNICATE A COMPELLING
BRAND PROMISE

"What's a brand? A singular idea that you own inside the mind of the prospect."
—AL RIES

"I am not looking like Armani today and somebody else tomorrow. I look like Ralph Lauren. And my goal is to consistently move in fashion and move in style without giving up what I am."
—RALPH LAUREN

Brands are one of the most powerful tools in the arsenal of the salesperson. In our book *The New Elite*, we posed the following thought experiment: Suppose you could own all aspects of Mercedes-Benz—the manufacturing plants, the distribution pipeline, the dealerships, and the customers. Or you could own the name Mercedes-Benz. Which would you choose? Of course, you would choose the name. All the physical assets of the company could reliably be replicated in relatively short order with enough money. The name, however, and all the rich emotional connections with it, could be reconstructed only with decades of effort, dedication, and consistent performance.

Branding is important in two realms. Most obviously, there is the brand of what you are selling or the company you represent. And then there is your own brand, as a person and a professional. Communicating both brands in a compelling way is a key strategy for enhancing your sales. Ideally, the meaning of a brand—what we call the brand promise—can be conveyed in a single word or phrase. For example, in the minds of most people, "Volvo" and "safety" are synonymous. Similarly, "BMW" *is* "finely engineered" and "Apple" *is* "innovative design." Can you capture the essence of your brand in a single word or phrase?

Great brand promises, be they for corporate brands or for individual salespeople, are built upon three key elements.

1. *Truth*. The brand promise must be inarguably, factually correct. It must stem from one's strengths and passions. Volvo, for example, can make safety

the core of its brand promise because the company's products are, in fact, demonstrably safe, with a heritage of safety innovations built into their corporate DNA. To prospects, untrue brand promises will be patently obvious and come across as inauthentic.

2. *Meaning.* A brand promise must be meaningful to clients and prospects. It must speak to their needs and be consistent with their values and passions. Safety in a car doesn't speak to everyone, but it is meaningful to the folks that Volvo targets.

3. *Distinctiveness.* The ideal brand promise is unique to that brand and stands out from the competitors' promises.

EXERCISES

- Make a list of what is true, meaningful, and distinctive about (a) the brands you sell/represent, and (b) you as a sales professional.

- Distill the meaning of your brand down to a single word or phrase.

- Practice communicating your brand essence to prospects and customers.

EXPRESSION 11:
HONE A COMPELLING ELEVATOR PITCH

"Communication works for those who work at it."
—John Powell

We hope you are passionate about your job. Or you're working to get there. Or you've set out to find out what your passion is and what the environment is that would be a good fit. That's great. But it's not enough.

You've got to be able to communicate that passion in ways that are authentic and engaging. Expressing the love for your job is a good start. But a compelling elevator pitch is just as important. We've all heard the concept: Imagine you're in an elevator with someone, and you've got thirty seconds to explain who you are and what your business proposition is. That is, your elevator pitch should be pithy and punchy, packed with benefits. You can find books and Web sites devoted to creating and refining one. But here's how you can create the most influential elevator pitch: Make sure it touches all three passions discussed in this book (a sincere love for what you do, alignment with your prospect's pursuit of a sincere interest, and the transcendent nature of your offering). Here's a very simple but very effective example:

> *"I sell Mercedes for Smith Dealership. I've always been passionate about cars, and I love working for Smith because they have a fifty-year history of really taking care of customers. Legendary Mercedes cars, happy customers . . . I'm a lucky guy."*

Now let's take a look at Figure 5.1 to see what makes this pitch effective.

FIGURE 5.1
An Effective Elevator Pitch

"I sell Mercedes for Smith Dealership." →	Simple language. Easily understood. Nothing high falutin. No industry jargon. And it mentions two brand names in the first six words.
"I've always been passionate about cars, and . . ." →	Expresses long-term passion for the product.
"I love working for Smith because . . ." →	Expresses love of job. Mentions and reinforces the distinctiveness of the dealer brand ("I don't love working for just anybody—Smith is different").
"They have a fifty-year history of really taking care of customers." →	Specific detail that reinforces brand distinctiveness, quality, and service.
"Legendary Mercedes cars, happy customers . . . I'm a lucky guy." →	Reinforces the product brand and speaks to happiness in two ways—as something you deliver, and as something you are. Both ways, it makes people want to be around you.

The example elevator pitch in Figure 5.1 is short, but it grabs attention, conveys a tremendous amount, and speaks to all three passions. Now, it's time to polish yours.

EXERCISES

- Draft your elevator pitch with passion, brands, and happiness at the core.

- Refine your elevator pitch based on feedback from friends and colleagues.

- Practice your elevator pitch until it feels natural and authentic.

EXPRESSION 12:
ASK PASSION-BASED QUESTIONS

"If you want a wise answer, ask a reasonable question."
—JOHANN WOLFGANG VON GOETHE

*"A sudden bold and unexpected question doth
many times surprise a man and lay him open."*
—FRANCIS BACON

Books on sales methods are fond of teaching the art of asking questions. And for good reason. Asking questions and listening to the answers are crucial steps to the sales process. Sometimes attempts to manipulate the question-asking process can be taken to extreme lengths. We saw in an earlier chapter just how many decades those classic sales questioning techniques have been around, like asking questions that lead to patterns of affirmative responses or asking leading questions like "What color do you want it in?" rather than "Do you want it?"

We'd like to add a subtlety to the extensive literature on asking sales questions: the passion-based question. This simply means asking questions like a true enthusiast. It's about letting down your guard. It is less about crafting carefully worded questions designed to elicit a specific response, and more about sharing your passion in a way that is spontaneous and sincere. And these questions have the added benefit of nearly always generating a positive response in a natural and authentic way. Who can resist questions such as:

- Do you want to see something very cool?

- Do you want to see something you can't see anywhere else?

- You know what I'm into these days?

- You want to know what really makes this brand different from other ones?

- Do you want to see something truly exceptional about this product?

- You know what first excited me about this business?

- You know what my first car was? (appropriate for auto salesmen with interesting stories to tell about their love of their first car)

EXERCISE

Craft some passion-based questions that you can use to deepen your interactions with customers and prospects.

EXPRESSION 13:
SELL TO HAPPINESS

Even during the most challenging economic times since the Great Depression, happiness has been on the rise among the affluent, and nearly seven in ten now describe themselves as very happy (see Figure 5.2). It is not a happiness of self-delusion or escapism. It is a solid happiness, with strong psychological foundations. For example, 76 percent of those we surveyed felt highly successful in their personal lives (our general population surveys suggest that only half of the public at large feel highly successful). It is, in a sense, a rational exuberance. This is not a denial of today's economic problems but, rather, the confidence that results from challenges well met. For example, 72 percent of the affluent sampled agree with the statement: "I have become a much smarter shopper thanks to today's economic situation."

FIGURE 5.2
Percentages of the Affluent Who Describe
Themselves as Very Happy, 2007–2010

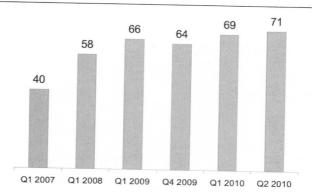

Harrison Group and American Express Publishing, *Survey of Affluence and Wealth in America*, 2010.

Here's the key: Today's affluent consumers do not buy to become happy; they buy *because* they are happy.

One way to sell to happiness is simply to be happy yourself. This simple act pulls together several of the techniques we have discussed in this chapter. Happiness is an extension of expressing the love you have for your job, and your sincere love of your life. And happiness is perhaps the most important characteristic you can share with your prospects. Revel in their happiness, too. Try to take it even further. As one of our wealthy research participants put it:

> *"I'm very passionate about putting forth the best for other people. Other people's happiness is as important to me as my own. And when they come to my business, my winery, and they tell*

me they had just the greatest time—that is the biggest motiva-tor to me. To continue to put forth the effort to make people come out and go 'wow'—that's motivating to me. I'm very passionate about that. If I sell crap wine . . . I could be success-ful and make a lot of money if that's success to you. But when you make a product from start to finish and grow it and make it and mold it and massage it and kiss it, just do everything you do from start to finish, you're giving it your all."

EXERCISES

- Be happy.

- Express your happiness.

- Understand what would make your customers even happier.

THE NEXT STEP

You've read our top thirteen ways of expressing passion in a selling context. We're sure there are many more possibilities (send us an e-mail—we'd love to hear yours). But for now, read on to the next chapter—about how to set goals and structure your work to maximize your ability to follow through and succeed.

CHAPTER SIX

From
Passion to
Execution

> "*If one advances confidently in the direction of his dreams, and endeavors to live that life which he has imagined, he will meet with success unexpected in common hours. If you have built castles in the air, your work need not be lost; that is where they should be. Now put the foundations under them.*"
> —HENRY DAVID THOREAU

Consider the full range of suggestions we have made for anyone aspiring to be a top sales performer, as shown in Figure 6.1.

FIGURE 6.1

Blueprint for Top Sales Performance

Foundations of Passion

Discover and Nurture Your Passions

Discover your strengths and passions. Rediscover lost ones.
Pursue them. Indulge them. Follow where they lead you.
If you aren't passionate about your job, then get passionate.
Improve the fit, or get a new job.

Understand the Passions of Prospects and Customers

Take a "passion census" of your customers. Really get
to understand their needs, businesses, and family lives.
Write a personal ad describing your target in detail.
Identify and frequent the "watering hole" communities
that might attract your target.

Leverage the Passion in the Product

Redouble your efforts to be a student of what you sell.
Be a student of your category, your industry, and your
competitors. Understand the expressions of excellence
and passion in them.

Expressions of Passion

Express the love of your job

Tell detail-rich stories

Discover a shared pursuit

Give the docent's tour

Understand their ultimate passion: family

Satisfy the passion du jour: value

Use the language of passion

Understand that reliability is "the new trust"

Create a ritual of celebration

Communicate a compelling brand promise

Hone a compelling elevator pitch

Ask passion-based questions

Sell to happiness

There's always room to improve. Even top performers will benefit from revisiting their current efforts in these areas and further sharpening their skills. For sales professionals with a more modest track record, these suggestions can become a roadmap for dramatically improving their performance. But the unfortunate reality is that most people will not improve. Most will read this book, give it some thought, take action in one or two modest ways, and return to the comfort zone of their old way of doing things. That's the unfortunate truth for much of the multimillion-dollar sales training industry.

WHY MOST SALES PROGRAMS FAIL

People routinely return from sales seminars and workshops pumped up, often with armloads of workbooks and motivational MP3s. But all too often that enthusiasm fades soon thereafter. They may have taken some notes on crafting a more compelling elevator pitch, but they don't practice that new pitch until it becomes part of their new and improved verbal repertoire. They make a dozen halfhearted efforts of the same sort, but the old patterns of thought and behavior reemerge, and they end up getting the same results they always got.

We have seen this happen in company after company. Considerable time, effort, and expense are put forth in carefully selecting a new matriculating class of salespeople. In a sales boot camp they are immersed in the subject. They are taught the ins and outs of their product line. They are given personality tests to identify their strengths and interests. They are handed sales scripts and told of ways to overcome objections; they are coached on their elevator pitches. They are given the steps for prospecting and building their pipeline. They now have the blueprint for their success. And the vast majority won't follow it.

Some simply lack the passion. They don't follow through on what they have learned and subsequent poor performance, job dissatisfaction, and turnover become part of their process of eventually discovering their passions and where those passions might fit. It's a painful process for everyone involved: expensive for the employer in terms of underperforming sales and wasted money, and expensive for the employee in terms of emotional turmoil and wasted time.

But the problem isn't always a lack of *passion*. It's often a lack of understanding about how best to execute a plan based on that passion. Like hopeless romantics and absentminded professors, these middle-of-the-pack performers may have a passion and lofty goals, but they get distracted, or disdain the hard work, or lack the stick-to-itiveness to rebound after setbacks. In contrast, top performers are characterized by a sense of passion, to be sure, but also by a determination and effectiveness in execution. We pointed out earlier that passion is a necessary but not sufficient condition for success. It drives results not through some mystical New Agey think-it-

and-it-will-happen process of manifestation, but because it so often inspires considerable, consistent, and effective action. Often, but not always.

Here's a selling secret: *Top performers are distinct not only for their passion but also because they do a host of little things that make it more likely they will be able to initiate and sustain those patterns of effective action.*

COMPARE WEIGHT LOSS
TO SALES PERFORMANCE

Consider the parallels in weight loss—yes, weight loss. As with sales performance, the vast majority of people who try to lose weight aren't terribly successful in the effort. But a few are, and their actions yield important clues to the nature of success.

After years of seemingly contradictory findings and conflicting dietary advice, a growing body of research has started to unlock the "secrets" of successful weight-loss maintenance, much of it conducted with the National Weight Control Registry, a database of individuals who have lost at least thirty pounds and kept it off for at least a year.[1] The findings reinforce the idea that there's only one fundamental rule to lasting weight loss: Burn off more calories than you consume. But people who maintain their weight loss do a host of little things differently that make it *more likely* they can balance the calories-in-versus-calories-out equation. These successful people do the following:

- Exercise more (averaging an hour a day).

- Weigh themselves more often.

- Usually eat breakfast every day (preventing diet-derailing midday hunger pangs).

- Have more social support.

- Stick to their eating and exercise regimens during the week and on weekends.

- Minimize the temptations in their environment.

- Find ways to cope effectively with stress and negative emotions.

- Effectively manage minor lapses, ensuring that they don't snowball into total collapses.

- Set goals for themselves more frequently and more effectively.

The difference between maintaining one's weight and regaining any weight lost is in part motivation (i.e., passion), to be sure, but also executional strategies. The same is true of the difference between top sales performers and their less productive counterparts.

But here's the most interesting thing about this list of success enhancers: With the exception of eating breakfast and weighing yourself frequently, every item on the list has been shown to enhance sales performance as well. Besides the obvious physical benefits, exercise boosts your mood, reduces stress, and is associated with stronger academic and career performance. Those with strong networks of social support live longer, healthier, more productive, and more satisfying lives. In fact, social support doesn't just "predict" these outcomes: It has a causal effect as well, even after controlling for preexisting physical conditions, income, age, education, smoking, drinking, exercise, blood pressure, cholesterol, access to health services, and satisfaction with life.

The essence of engaging in consistent, productive action—in other words, effective execution—is not particularly domain-specific. The same ideas and processes that lead to success in one area tend to be effective in others because they both have the ability to shape your life and life outcomes toward your passions.

SEVEN PRINCIPLES FOR MAKING IT HAPPEN

We'd like to end this book by sharing seven key principles for implementation and execution. Besides embracing passions, these are the defining characteristics that we have noted of top performers that keep them moving forward, that keep them from becoming idle dreamers and hopeless romantics who are full of passion but accomplish little.

1. *Be bold.* In most sales organizations, there are a handful of top performers who outsell the average performer—by a lot. Typically, they're not selling 5 or 10 *percent* more. They're selling five or ten *times* more. In meeting with them, we found it obvious that such a level of performance is important to them. Really important. They *want it*, and they recognize that dramatic action is required to achieve it. In a word, they're bold. They're not timid. We saw in Chapter 2 how these top performers are not necessarily life-of-the-party extraverts, but they're hardly shy about taking action. They're also not shy about telling people about their goals and ambitions—not to brag, but as a tool for keeping themselves accountable.

2. *Be lucky.* "I'm a great believer in luck, and I find that *the harder I work*, the more luck I have." This thought has been attributed to everyone from Thomas Jefferson and Benjamin Franklin to movie mogul Samuel Goldwyn. The sentiment has been around for centuries longer, because it conveys a fundamental truth. These days, there's a growing body of research revealing that, in fact, successful people are luckier than others. We reviewed much of this research in *The New Elite*, but for now we briefly mention one study in particular. People who considered themselves especially lucky and those who considered themselves especially unlucky were both given the task of looking through a newspaper and counting the number of photographs. On the second page of the newspaper, an entire half page had the headline "Stop Counting—There Are 43

Photographs in This Newspaper." Lucky people saw the headline; those who considered themselves unlucky missed it. Dr. Richard Wiseman, author of this study, put it this way:

> The harder they looked, the less they saw.
> And so it is with luck—unlucky people miss chance opportunities because they are too focused on looking for something else. They go to parties intent on finding their perfect partner and so miss opportunities to make good friends. They look through newspapers determined to find certain types of job advertisements and as a result miss other types of jobs. Lucky people are more relaxed and open, and therefore see what is there rather than just what they are looking for.[2]

Their boldness and higher activity level create more opportunities for top performers, and the openness that comes with their sense of luck makes sure that they see those opportunities as such. Pasteur was right: "Chance favors the prepared mind."

3. *Be curious.* Curiosity is the key to truly understanding your customers and prospects. Curiosity is also the lens through which you can spot trends, in both your industry and among your prospects and customers. You have to *want* to know: How are they feeling *right now*? What has been their path in life? What is it that makes them want to buy new china (or whatever) right now? When in doubt, we use these questions to facilitate our own sense of curiosity:

- What made you successful?

- How are you keeping yourself happy as a family in these tough times?

- What is it that makes purchasing so important right now?

- What can I do to help bring this to a close?

- What information and details would you really like to know?

Only by asking key questions and celebrating the answers can we have trends in our headlights, not in our taillights.

4. *Seize opportunities in the moment.* Seizing opportunities in the moment requires luck (seeing the opportunity), curiosity (exploring the opportunity), and boldness (taking action when the opportunity presents itself). All of these combine to produce a tendency to seize opportunities in the moment. At virtually every one of our training seminars we've heard the same story: One day, a prospect arrives (in the store, in the showroom, in your office, etc.). At first glance, for lack of a better word, the prospect is a bit . . . scruffy. In clothing and demeanor, this prospect just doesn't seem to fit the typical profile. And when most of the sales associates look the other way, a top performer takes the chance and seizes the opportunity in the moment. And boldness is rewarded. He or she ends

up getting a big sale (and usually a long-term customer), when others were turned off by first impressions.

Seizing opportunities in the moment requires *being* in the moment. You might be talking with your five hundredth prospect of the month, but for a new prospect, it is his or her first interaction with you. The individual wants to be evaluated for his or her own uniqueness, not through the lens of "customer number 501." Be in the moment with each prospect.

5. *Be a guide.* We touched on this idea in Chapter 5, with the concept of a docent-led tour. Customers and prospects today want a knowledgeable guide. Sometimes, this guiding is literal—walking a customer through a store or dealership. But you can also be a guide through a complex purchase process. Consider, for example, the 4 Cs of diamonds: color, cut, clarity, and carat weight. By giving prospects a structure for thinking about the category, the 4 Cs provide a framework for making informed decisions about quality and value. Ask yourself: What are the 4 Cs of *your* category? How can you be a more effective guide through the process of making a purchase decision?

6. *Set goals.* Literally hundreds of studies—in sales, and in virtually every other aspect of life—have shown the performance-enhancing power of goals. It's important to separate fact from fiction, however. In many sales books, and at even more sales training programs, the tale is told of the "Yale Study of Goals." The story is simple. The 1953 graduating class at Yale was

interviewed. Three percent of the students had written specific goals for their futures. Twenty years later, that 3 percent were found to have higher net worth than the other 97 percent combined. It's a powerful story, but it turns out that the study is merely a "self-improvement urban legend." When asked for details or a write-up of the study, the well-known self-help gurus and self-appointed sales "experts" could produce nothing. They had simply heard it from each other, repeating the story until it became an accepted part of sales lore.[3]

Urban legends are repeated for a reason, and in this case, it's because the moral of the story is true: There is a deep underlying truth to the notion that setting goals can enhance success. But the research reveals a subtlety: The goals boost performance only if they are set and pursued in accordance with specific principles.[4] First and foremost—and from what we have already seen, no surprise—is this: People perform best when they set goals consistent with their passions, values, and interests. This alignment of goals and passions has been shown to lead to harder work and better performance, but it also leads to enjoying the process more—more interest, excitement, confidence, creativity, energy, and happiness.

There are other characteristics of the goals set by high-achieving people; for example, they tend to set challenging, specific, near-term goals. *Challenging* goals provide the motivation to work hard. *Specific* goals eliminate the wiggle room of rationalizing a lack of hard work with an "I never really set that goal anyway" response. And *near-term* goals are particularly powerful, as they harness the burst of activity that occurs as a goal looms, a phenomenon known as the *imminence effect.* Sometimes sales quotas are too big and too far into the future to be truly motivating. When this happens, top performers often improvise a series of near-term, pipeline-focused goals ("My annual goal of $5 million in sales is too far in the future, so I set weekly goals for myself in terms of phone calls made and leads generated.").

7. *Be happy.* We said it before, and it bears repeating: Be happy. In case you needed yet another reason, here's one: Happy people achieve more. You might expect that success comes first—achieve your goals, and then you'll get happy. In fact, more often than not, it is happiness that comes first. Happy people are more likely to find their passions, set more effective goals, work harder, and have more social support; the success comes as a result.[5]

A FINAL THOUGHT

In some of our sales training efforts, we give new sales associates the opportunity to spend time talking with top performers—a chance to learn at the feet of the master, as it were. Sometimes it is an insightful and motivating conversation for both. But too often, the new sales associates walk away from these conversations a little disappointed. They find the meeting disappointingly mundane. They were expecting to learn the *secrets* to sales success. They're not exactly sure what they expected those to be—some secret handshake, hypnotic power, bit of verbal jujitsu, or easy-assembly instructions for a long list of rich people who really, really want to buy stuff right now.

Instead what they heard often sounds a little unspectacular—and disappointingly like a lot of work. If they listened closely, they probably heard something like, "Figure out what you really want from life. Then go for it. Find a job and an environment that fit well with your passions and strengths. Take steps to make them fit even better. Work hard. Set goals."

Not glamorous advice on the surface, perhaps. But it is the best advice for anyone striving for success in sales. And in life. Finding one's passion, and leveraging the thirteen expressions of it, will energize you and those around you. By sharing your passion, you will find success in life, no matter what you are selling and no matter what you wish to accomplish.

Our Methodologies for Studying the Affluent and Wealthy

WHEN WE ADD UP THE INTERVIEWS, questionnaires, and focus groups we have conducted, and the successful people in business we have worked with in the process of building our understanding of America's wealthiest households, we realize that we have had the pleasure of speaking with over 10,000 people of means during the past half decade. This appendix briefly describes the methodologies we used in our larger quantitative studies.

Throughout our research, we have been fortunate to have sponsors who devoted their time and thoughtfulness in helping us refine our research, focus our sampling methodology, and fine-tune the implications for their specific categories. These sponsors have included AgencySacks, Bank of America, Bank of New York Mellon, Bombardier Flexjet, Cadillac, Cartier, Fairmont Hotels & Resorts, Fireman's Fund Insurance, Four Seasons Hotels and Resorts, Leading

Real Estate Companies of the World, Lexus, Louis Vuitton, Lyle Anderson, Maui Land & Pineapple Company, Mercedes-Benz, Neuberger Berman, Saks Fifth Avenue, Union Bank of California, and U.S. Trust.

THE SURVEY OF AFFLUENCE
AND WEALTH IN AMERICA

This survey was born in 2006, as a partnership between the market research and strategy firm Harrison Group and American Express Publishing, whose magazines include *Travel + Leisure*, *Food & Wine*, and *Departures*. The two firms embarked on a collective research effort to take an annual look at the attitudes, values, and preferences of today's affluent and wealthy, with three particular goals in mind:

1. To conduct a comprehensive study of the top 5 percent of American consumers, as defined by discretionary household income

2. To examine the different ways these people value their resources, time, and shopping experiences

3. To examine how brands, the shopping process, media, and personal experiences affect the way these consumers bring quality and value into their lives

Since its initial year, the research has broadened and deepened in scope. We have expanded our sampling frame to encompass the top 10 percent of the American financial elite, reflecting those Americans with at least $100,000 in annual discretionary income. As the economic downturn accelerated throughout 2008, we began conducting interviews quarterly to keep our finger on the pulse of rapidly changing attitudes. Starting in 2009, we began collecting data monthly. In 2010, for example, we began the year with a primary wave of data collection consisting of 1,442 interviews in January and February, followed by at least 200 interviews in each following month.

At its most granular and refined level, our sampling plan is based on four key economic strata defined in terms of discretionary income, which is operationally defined by starting with self-reported income and subtracting mortgage, taxes, children's educational expenses, and other expenses considered nondiscretionary. (Interestingly, our research has found that children's educational expenses are typically considered a must-have, nondiscretionary item.) Table A.1 shows the breakdown of financial resources (as of 2010) held by financially elite households, ranging from upper middle class through wealthy.

For the purposes of this book, we have condensed these four economic strata into two groups. We use the term *affluent* to refer to households with at least $100,000 in annual discretionary income; collectively, they represent the top 10 percent of the American financial elite, and this group comprises 10 to 11 million households. We use the term *wealthy* to apply to households with at least $500,000 a year in discretionary income. The wealthy represent roughly the top 0.6 percent of the U.S. financial elite, or approximately 680,000 households.

Defined in these ways, the affluent and the wealthy are highly similar in terms of background, attitudes, and overall approaches to the marketplace. Both groups are characterized as having middle-class backgrounds; middle-class mindsets; and a distinct quality-meets-value approach to purchasing, regardless of the price points involved. But in terms of their spending capabilities and proclivities, the wealthy are clearly a cut above. Most are members of the $1 million/$10 million club—$1 million in annual income and $10 million in assets.

TABLE A.1

**Income and Assets for
Higher-Income Households**

	Upper Middle Class	Affluent	Super Affluent	Wealthy
Discretionary income	$100–125K	$125–249K	$250–499K	$500+
Average income	$146K	$237K	$432K	$1.57MM
Average assets	$2.4MM	$3.2MM	$6.0MM	$12.4MM
# of households	6.3MM	2.5MM	1.5MM	680,000
% of U.S. households	5.7%	2.3%	1.4%	.6%

Source: Harrison Group and American Express Publishing, *Survey of Affluence and Wealth in America*, 2010.

FIGURE A.1

U.S. Asset Concentration

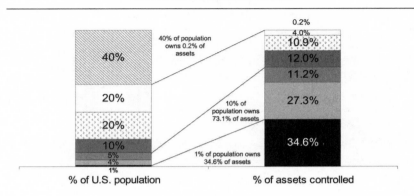

Source: E. N. Wolff, "Recent Trends in Household Wealth in the United States: Rising Debt and the Middle-Class Squeeze—An Update to 2007," *Working Paper No. 589* (Annandale-on-Hudson, N.Y.: Levy Economics Institute of Bard College, 2010); www.levyinstitute.org.

Growing Asset Concentration in the United States

Collectively, these small groups of financially successful people have tremendous financial resources and spending power. Government estimates suggest that the top 1 percent of U.S. financial elite (for example) account for one-third of all privately held assets in the United States. The top 5 percent are worth more financially than the other 95 percent combined. The top 20 percent control 85 percent of the assets. Essentially, the bottom 40 percent of households have no assets, living from paycheck to paycheck, if they are lucky (see Figure A.1).

These figures of net-worth concentration—the assets owned by the top 1 percent and top 5 percent of Americans—are near their highest in the past century, with the exception of a pre-Depression spike in 1929. As the figures show, a large proportion of the country's assets are held by a small number of wealthy individuals. An examination of trends in this distribution of income and assets over the past 100 years offers insights into the relative inequality of today's economic situation. During the mid-twentieth century, there was a greater dispersion of wealth in society, there was substantial growth of the middle class, and salary structures and tax regimes discouraged the accumulation of dramatic wealth. But that changed with the 1980s. For example:

- Personal income tax rates for the highest earners dropped substantially.

- More subtly but more important, changes in the tax laws encouraged new kinds of risk, unleashing a flood of capital into venture markets, enabling entrepreneurs to more easily gain funding for new ventures and providing faster accumulation of wealth.

- Corporate norms changed; impressive pay and stock option packages became de rigueur in the recruitment and retention of top executives.

- Social norms changed, with money taking the foreground—think yuppies and Gordon Gecko's "greed is good" speech in the movie *Wall Street*.

- The movement toward the "massification of luxury" began in earnest; traditional luxury brands began expanding awareness into "aspirational" segments, and expanding (some would say diluting) their product lines to include relatively low-priced but less than subtly branded accessories.

Collectively, the entire ethos of money in society changed, and a new generation of wealthy individuals emerged. The Rockefellers, Mellons, and other patrons of old-school money fell off the Forbes 400 List (which, in another sign of the growing concentration of wealth, became a billionaires-only list—mere millionaires need not apply). Their place was taken by the entrepreneurs, the senior executives, and the self-made of all stripes—those rising from middle-class backgrounds to bring a new perspective on money and all that a life of abundance brings with it. Hence the title of our first book, *The New Elite: Inside the Minds of the Truly Wealthy*. Figure A.2 shows the 1980s and 1990s saw steady growth of wealth held by the top 1 percent of Americans.

Data on income inequality are compiled and analyzed by the field's leading expert, Edward Wolff, of the Levy Economics Institute of Bard College. The data themselves, however, are largely taken from the Federal Reserve's *Surveys of Consumer Finances*, published every three years, most recently in 2007. As a result, precisely how the Great Recession may be shaping financial inequality is difficult to know with certainty. Certainly stock portfolios, which constitute a high percentage of the wealthy's assets, took a significant hit—often 30 to 40 percent or more. But at the same

FIGURE A.2

Percentage of U.S. Wealth Held by the Top 1 Percent of Americans

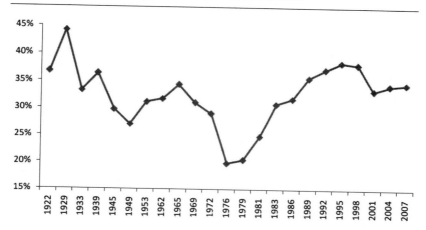

Source: E. N. Wolff, *Top Heavy* (New York: New Press, 1996); E. N. Wolff, "Recent Trends in Household Wealth in the United States: Rising Debt and the Middle-Class Squeeze—An Update to 2007," *Working Paper No. 589* (Annandale-on-Hudson, N.Y.: Levy Economics Institute of Bard College, 2010); www.levyinstitute.org.

time, housing prices, which constitute a greater portion of the assets of nonaffluent Americans, took a dramatic hit as well. There is evidence, however, that as 2010 inches (we hope) into a recovery, it is benefiting the wealthy disproportionately. Consider that from 2008 to 2010 mean income among the top 10 percent rose from $492,000 to $502,000, while median income is significantly lower and falling (from $325,000 to $275,000). And while assets are up among the affluent as a whole (from $4.2 million to $5 million), this increase is largely driven by the rise in assets among the wealthy, from $9.8 million to $12.4 million.

It is also clear that the recession has reshaped, in short order, the demographics of today's financial elite. Compared to 2008, today's affluent and wealthy are older, now averaging nearly fifty. And as a result, they are less likely to have kids under the age of eighteen in the household (only 41 percent, down from 50 percent just two years ago). They are more seasoned in life, but not necessarily more seasoned with wealth; on average, it has been only ten years since their first major liquidity event introduced them to the pleasures and challenges of living with abundance. Ethnically, today's affluent and wealthy have become a more homogeneous group, with 89 percent now being Caucasian. Most of the nonwhites are Asians (roughly half of whom live in California), while African Americans and Hispanics have seen their numbers among the financial elite dwindle, as Table A.2 shows.

Markets Are Moving to the Extremes

The returning interest in luxury can be better understood by looking closer at the shifts among key segments of the affluent and wealthy populations. This market can be viewed as consisting of three types of buyers: skeptics, diligents, and traditionals (see Figure A.3). Luxury has faced challenges over the past three years because the ranks of those skeptical about luxury and the value of luxury brands have swelled; just 19 percent of the upscale population in 2007, skeptics now constitute 34 percent, adding roughly 400,000 more households since 2009 alone. These "skeptics" are emphatic

TABLE A.2

Demographic Characteristics of the Affluent, 2008–2010

	2008 %	2009 %	2010 %
Age	46	47	**49**
Have a child under 18	**50**	46	41
White/ Caucasian	80	**88**	89
Mean income	**$492K**	$472K	**$506K**
Mean assets	$4.2	$4.0	**$5.0**
Tenure with wealth	**12.4 yrs**	9.7 yrs	**10.2 yrs**

Source: Harrison Group and American Express Publishing, *Survey of Affluence and Wealth in America*, 2010.

discount shoppers—they go to great lengths to avoid being defined by their money or by making ostentatious statements with their purchases.

At the other end of the spectrum, the returning interest in luxury is driven by traditional luxury shoppers, who have grown their ranks by 400,000 households in the past year. These "traditionals" personified the "I want" economy, translating their passions into purchases without hesitation or guilt. It was these shoppers who historically provided luxury retail outlets with their keystone margins, and it was their rapid disappearance from the marketplace that fundamentally reshaped retail two years ago.

Today, even though traditionals still number nearly 2 million fewer than just three years ago, their growing numbers in 2010, and their average luxury spending of $331,000 per person per year, presents significant opportunities for luxury retailers. In fact, spending from these traditionals alone will likely offset net spending declines from other segments, and will power modest near-term growth in the luxury market as a whole.

OPTIMISM CONTINUES ITS CAUTIOUS RETURN

The first quarter of 2010 saw a significant improvement in overall optimism among the affluent and wealthy. The second quarter of 2010 has established this improvement as a

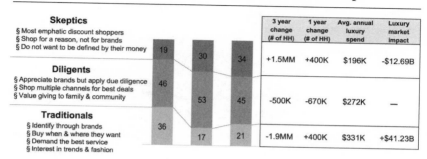

FIGURE A.3

Changes in Three Wealthy Consumer Groups

		3 year change (# of HH)	1 year change (# of HH)	Avg. annual luxury spend	Luxury market impact
Skeptics · Most emphatic discount shoppers · Shop for a reason, not for brands · Do not want to be defined by their money	19 / 30 / 34	+1.5MM	+400K	$196K	-$12.69B
Diligents · Appreciate brands but apply due diligence · Shop multiple channels for best deals · Value giving to family & community	46 / 53 / 45	-500K	-670K	$272K	—
Traditionals · Identify through brands · Buy when & where they want · Demand the best service · Interest in trends & fashion	36 / 17 / 21	-1.9MM	+400K	$331K	+$41.23B

definite trend, if a slow and cautious one. For the first time since the first quarter of 2008, optimism in people's futures and their children's futures has reached the 55 percent mark. Optimism about the future of America and the world lag far behind but are trending up as well and have nearly doubled since their fourth-quarter 2009 lows (see Figure A.4).

While optimism continues to rise, the once palpable economic fears are dropping and the first-quarter improvements in "financial worry" metrics have largely maintained themselves in the second quarter. A still substantial 38 percent of people fear running out of money, down substantially from the 48 percent observed as recently as the fourth quarter of 2009. People's worries about losing their job and about their company's survival are also below their 2009 highs (see Figure A.5).

FIGURE A.4

Percentages of the Affluent Who Are Optimistic, Quarterly 2008–2010

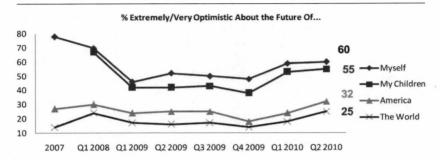

FIGURE A.5

Changes in Levels of Concern Among the Affluent, 2008–2010

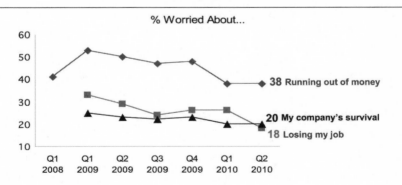

A FRAGILE OPTIMISM, WEAKENED BY STOCK MARKET CONCERNS

Signs abound that today's optimism is experiencing a cautious and tentative return. Almost universally, the wealthy we surveyed continue to believe that the United States is in a recession. Federal Reserve Board Chairman Ben Bernanke's September 2009 statement that "The recession is very likely over at this point" had little impact on the psyches or spending habits of the affluent. Sixty-one percent expect the recession to last longer than a year, a distressingly high number that continues to inch up. This is made even more remarkable by the fact that the Great Recession was by far the longest and most severe downturn of the post-WWII era (see Table A.3).

The sheer length of the recession continues to take its psychological toll. The National Bureau of Economic Research tells us that the recession formally began in December 2007 and ended in June 2009. But for consumers, the recession "emotionally" began in 2006 and continues today. In other words, *they've lived with a recessionary mindset and shopping repertoire for four years, and they expect it to last at least another year* (see Figure A.6). They've braced themselves for the long haul. Moreover, their reactions (including more prudent spending and a heightened value orientation) are no longer new—they are refined and well honed.

TABLE A.3
Major U.S. Recessions

Dates of Recession	# of months
Nov 1948–Oct 1949	11
July 1953–May 1954	10
Aug 1957–April 1958	8
April 1960–Feb 1961	10
Dec 1969–Feb 1970	11
Nov 1973–March 1975	16
Jan 1980–July 1980	6
July 1981–Nov 1982	16
July 1990–March 1991	8
March 2001–Nov 2001	8
Dec 2007–June 2009	18

Source: National Bureau of Economic Research, http://www.nber.org/cycles/cycle
main.html (accessed September 9, 2010).

FIGURE A.6

Outlooks of the Affluent Regarding the Recession

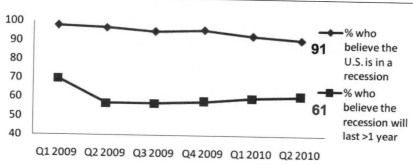

Today's mildly resurgent optimism could easily be derailed by any number of economic, political, or personal events. A declining stock market is obviously one such scenario that shows distressing signs of emerging. Confidence that the stock market will "bounce back soon" (a measure that closely tracks actual market performance) has dropped to its 2010 lows, having slid 13 percentage points during the second quarter alone (see Figure A.7). Confidence in the real estate market has also slid, essentially reaching the 50/50 point after peaking at 60 percent in March. Taken as a whole, both metrics are well above their first-quarter 2009 lows but have settled back toward their less than inspiring averages of the past two years.

FIGURE A.7

Percentage of the Affluent Who
Believe Stock Markets Will Rise

% believing each market will "bounce back soon"

—◆—Stock Market   —■—Real Estate Market

SPENDING CUTBACKS STILL PREVALENT

The "return" of consumer spending is as fragile and halting as the return of optimism. It's still premature to say that affluent consumers as a whole have increased their spending. Instead, it continues to be more accurate to say that the majority are still cutting back, but not as big a majority compared to a year ago. Consider that 64 percent of the affluent continue looking closely at their spending in every category, and 61 percent report buying fewer big-ticket items than a year ago. Both metrics have declined consistently over the

FIGURE A.8

**Measures of Financial Concern and
Spending Cutbacks, 2008–2010**

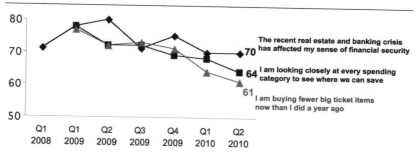

past eighteen months, each losing about 15 percentage points. But both obviously remain high in absolute terms. Moreover, seven in ten surveyed—unchanged from 2008— express being shaken by today's economic situation (see Figure A.8).

Overall spending projections reflect the ambivalence and uncertainty of today's consumers. For the past year, the numbers of those expecting to increase their spending have been held in check by roughly the same numbers expecting to decrease spending. This is a significant improvement from early 2008, when the number of decreasers outnumbered the increasers by four to one, but obviously not indicative of an impending growth spurt. Hybrid automobiles and children's clothing show clear signs of growth, with spending on vacations and weekend getaways showing signs of at least breaking even. Fashion-related categories, however, show signs of continued challenges (see Table A.4 and Figure A.9).

TABLE A.4
Projected Spending Changes (by category)

	Q1 2010 %	Q2 2010 %
Hybrid automobile	7	8
Children's clothing	3	5
Weekend getaways	0	4
Family car	2	2
SUV	0	1
Vacations	−1	0
Home décor and furnishings	−3	0
Home electronics	−3	−1

Footwear	−2	−2
Eating in restaurants	−4	−2
Private jet usage	−3	−4
Apparel/Fashion	−5	−4
Personal leather goods	−9	−6
Accessories	−8	−6
Business travel	−3	−6
Resorts and fine hotels	−8	−6
Handbags	−9	−7
Jewelry	−14	−9

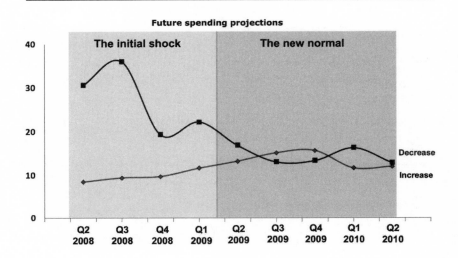

FIGURE A.9

Projected Spending Changes, 2008–2010

FINDING STRENGTH AND HAPPINESS
AMID ECONOMIC UNCERTAINTY

Despite the affluent's continuing economic concerns, cautious approach to spending, and tenuous sense of optimism, their happiness continues its seemingly improbable rise. As we described in Chapter 5, a sense of "rational exuberance" has taken hold, with pervasive feelings of success and happiness actually rising. It's been the result of confidence from challenges well met, a heightened sense of priorities, and a redoubled focus on family. Considering that, among the affluent . . .

- 89 percent agree: "I have done a good job of making my household more fiscally responsible."

- 77 percent agree: "Because of the recession, I have become a more resourceful person."

- 75 percent agree: "Because of the economy, I am talking about money with my children."

- 73 percent agree: "I have become a much smarter shopper, thanks to today's economic situation."

- 64 percent agree: "My significant other and I have learned to work together because of the economy."

It has been a remarkable shift in mindset. When the money was flowing, when it seemed that everybody was thriving financially, whatever money or success people had didn't feel like enough. It still felt like "everybody else" was getting rich. The media obliged with plenty of stories to reinforce that perception. Social comparisons skewed upward; the affluent mentally compared themselves to wealthier individuals or those whose businesses had grown more dramatically, and they felt bad about their own accomplishments as a result. Today, social comparisons skew downward, with the affluent mentally comparing themselves to the less fortunate.

Nearly half of the U.S. population has been personally impacted by the economy, whether through a job loss, a salary reduction, or reduced hours, meaning that most affluent people know more than one person who has been personally touched by the recession. Today's affluent feel fortunate for their business success and their solid financial standing—in a very real sense, they are proud to be still standing. They feel smart and resourceful, not fearful or deprived. They have found that consumption and acquisition are easier to do without than they had expected. And on top of that, the economic challenges have brought their families closer together. Little wonder they are feeling not only happier but also more successful.

KEY TAKE-AWAYS AND THE OUTLOOK FOR THE FUTURE

Here are some key points to consider for the immediate future.

- *Expect that affluent spending will continue to be suppressed.* As this book goes to press in late 2010, we forecast that net spending in 2010 by the affluent will be 1 to 2 percent below an obviously weak 2009. Many scenarios present themselves that could undermine today's returning optimism, but even the rosiest scenarios of economic recovery are unlikely to spur a return to the enthusiasm for consumption and acquisition we witnessed in the mid-2000s. Marketing should maintain its subdued and understated tone, and companies should continue to manage inventory carefully.

- *The "we need" categories will see modest growth.* Although spending will go down overall, more dramatic will be the shifts in spending across categories. Signs of growth are evident in the categories that speak to the needs of family, or reinforce the family's collective sense of resourcefulness or their broader desire to "do the right thing" during challenging times. Family travel, clothes and other necessities for the kids, and hybrid automobiles will show growth. Fashion in its various incarnations—including apparel, accessories, handbags, and jewelry—will continue to be challenged.

- *Look for toes to be dipped back into luxury waters.* While consumption has yet to rebound, logo shame and the "embarrassment" of wealth show distinct signs of receding. A growing number "kind of like it" when they are recognized as being wealthy, while the guilt associated with luxury purchases has waned. Interest in luxury is trending up modestly, while the tendency to deny oneself luxury is trending downward. Luxury purchases will be few and carefully thought out. They may be small, but they will be meaningful in their emotional and symbolic impact.

- *Cater to self-reliant consumers.* Trust in institutions has been low for decades. But over the past few years, confidence in salespeople in particular has fallen. In both product knowledge and personal relationships, disappointment is rising and the expectations the affluent have of sales situations have dropped.

For companies, there are opportunities both to deliver higher-quality sales interactions and to enable self-service opportunities for the growing numbers who would rather bypass salespeople altogether.

- *Leverage the new value equation.* Value orientation remains tremendously strong. And the emphasis now is on value given price, rather than the other way around. Communicating lasting value—in a sense, being investment grade, no matter your category— is crucial to resonating with today's affluent consumers.

THE SURVEY OF AFFLUENT ATTITUDES TOWARD SALESPEOPLE

In June 2010, we conducted another survey, this one on affluent people's attitudes toward salespeople. This fifteen-minute online survey inquired about the wealthy's general attitudes toward salespeople, their perceptions of salespeople in different industries, and their purchase preferences across categories. It also included unstructured, open-ended questions whereby respondents were asked to describe their best and worst experiences with salespeople while purchasing high-end or luxury items. In total, 1,037 individuals participated in the survey; unless otherwise noted, data cited in this book are from the 404 respondents with at least $125,000 in annual income.

The survey was conducted in conjunction with the Ambassadors Network, a network of over 20,000 upscale customers of American Express Publishing's magazines, Web sites, affinity clubs, and books. The Ambassadors are united in their desire to share their ideas and opinions, to engage with brands that are relevant to them, and to learn about new innovations and market trends. For marketers, the Ambassador's Network serves as a high-speed, low-cost, high-quality way of communicating with trusted brand advisers about brands; categories; new product ideas; advertising campaigns; and, of course, opinions about salespeople. (For more information about the Ambassadors Network, visit www.ambassadorsnet.com.)

THE SURVEY OF AMERICAN ATTITUDES TOWARD THE WEALTHY

In 2006, Harrison Group conducted a nationally representative survey to understand how Americans view the wealthy. Conducted online with over 1,000 respondents, the research focused on how Americans believe the wealthy acquired their money and the personality traits they believe are common among wealthy individuals.

Notes

Chapter One:
The Desire to Acquire

1. Dr. Brosnan, quoted in Charles Q. Choi, "Chimps Act Like Humans: Mine! Mine! Mine!" *LiveScience*, posted October 8, 2007, at http://www.livescience.com/animals/071008-chimp-endowment.html; accessed September 7, 2010. The research by Dr. Brosnan and her colleagues was published in "Endowment Effects in Chimpanzees," *Current Biology* 17 (2007): 1704–7; see http://www.cell.com/current-biology/abstract/S0960-9822(07)01915-X.

2. John Dawes, "Price Changes and Defection Levels in a Subscription-Type Market," *Journal of Services Marketing* 18, no. 1 (2004): 35–44.

3. For a definitive history of sales in America, see Walter Friedman, *Birth of a Salesman* (Cambridge, Mass.: Harvard University Press, 2005).

4. For a more detailed history of luxury, see Christopher Berry, *The Idea of Luxury: A Conceptual and Historical Investigation* (Cambridge, England: Cambridge University Press, 1994).

5. From Juvenal's *Satires*, quoted in Berry, *Idea of Luxury*, p. 69.

6. Tacitus, *The Agricola* (London: Loeb Library, 1924), chap. 21, p. 690.

7. Naphtali Lewis and Meyer Reinhold, *Roman Civilization: Selected Readings*, Volume 1 (Cambridge, England: Cambridge University Press, 1990), p. 439.

Chapter Two:
The Passion of the Salesperson

1. Richard Behar Dallas, "Ross Perot's Days at Big Blue," *Time*, July 20, 1992; http://www.time.com/time/magazine/article/0,9171,976048-1,00.html; accessed September 8, 2010.

2. "Ross Perot: The Billionaire Boy Scout," *Entrepreneur*, October 10, 2008; available http://www.entrepreneur.com/growyourbusiness/radicalsandvisionaries/article197682.html; accessed September 8, 2010.

3. Dallas, "Ross Perot's Days."

4.   Ebenezer Hannaford, *Success in Canvassing: A Practical Manual of Hints and Instructions, Specifically Adapted to the Use of Book Canvassers of the Better Class* (St. Louis, Mo.: N.D. Thompson, 1875; revised 1884).

5.   Abraham Cahan, *The Rise of David Levinsky* (Whitefish, Mont.: Kessinger, 1917/2004), p. 283.

6.   Matt Oechsli, *The Art of Selling to the Affluent: How to Attract, Service, and Retain Wealthy Customers and Clients for Life* (Hoboken, N.J.: John Wiley, 2005), p. 202.

7.   Remy Stern, *But Wait . . . There's More! Tighten Your Abs, Make Millions, and Learn How the $100 Billion Infomercial Industry Sold Us Everything but the Kitchen Sink* (New York: HarperCollins, 2009), p. 4.

8.   Charles Wilson Hoyt, *Scientific Sales Management: A Practical Application of the Principles of Scientific Management to Selling* (New York: Charles B. Woolson, 1918), p. 26.

9.   "The Science of Selling," *NCR*, August 1, 1903, p. 529.

10.   *NCR*, July 1, 1902, p. 409.

11.   Elsie Oschrin, "Vocational Tests for Retail Saleswomen," *Journal of Applied Psychology* 2 (1918): 148–55.

12.   Gilbert A. Churchill, Jr., et al., "The Determinants of Salesperson Performance: A Meta-Analysis," *Journal of Marketing Research* 22 (May 1985): 103–18.

13.   Ibid., p. 104.

14. For example, see Robert Rosenthal et al., *Contrasts and Effect Sizes in Behavioral Research* (Cambridge, England: Cambridge University Press, 2000).

15. Fernando Jaramillo et al., "A Meta-Analysis of the Relationship Between Organizational Commitment and Salesperson Job Performance: 25 Years of Research," *Journal of Business Research* 58 (2005): 705–14.

16. Data and conclusions in this paragraph are from Murray R. Barrick and Michael K. Mount, "The Big Five Personality Dimension and Job Performance: A Meta-Analysis," *Personnel Psychology* 44 (1991): 1–26.

17. Martin Seligman, *Learned Optimism: How to Change Your Mind and Your Life* (New York: Vintage, 2006).

18. Andrew J. Vinchur, Jeffery S. Schippmann, Fred S. Switzer III, and Philip L. Roth, "A Meta-Analytic Review of Predictors of Job Performance for Salespeople," *Journal of Applied Psychology* 83 (1998): 586–97.

19. Tony Rutigliano and Benson Smith, *Discover Your Sales Strengths: How the World's Greatest Salespeople Develop Winning Careers* (New York: Random House, 2003), p. 8.

20. Ibid., p. 15.

21. "Strength-Based Development: Using Strength to Accelerate Performance"; http://www. Gallup.com/consulting/61/strengths-development.asps; accessed September 8, 2010.

22. "Employee Engagement Report, 2008"; http://blessingwhite.com/eee_report.asp; accessed September 8, 2010.

23. "Employee Engagement: A Leading Indicator of Financial Performance"; http://www.gallup.com/consulting/52/employee-engagement.asps; accessed September 8, 2010.

24. For example, David Myers, *The Pursuit of Happiness: What Makes a Person Happy and Why* (New York: William Morrow, 1992).

25. Quoted in Michael Torrice, "Want Passionate Kids? Leave 'em Alone," *LiveScience*; http://www.livescience.com/culture/children-passions-autonomy-100209.html; posted February 9, 2010; accessed September 9, 2010.

26. Nalini Ambady et al., "The 30-Sec Scale: Using Thin-Slice Judgments to Evaluate Sales Effectiveness," *Journal of Consumer Psychology* 16 (2005): 4–13.

27. For a review of Dr. Dweck's work, see Carol Dweck and Ellen Leggett, "A Social-Cognitive Approach to Motivation and Personality," *Psychological Review* 95 (1988): 256–73. Conclusions in this chapter about how a learning orientation improves sales performance are detailed in Don VandeWalle, Steven P. Brown, William L. Cron, and John W. Slocum, Jr., "The Influence of Goal Orientation and Self-Regulation Tactics on Sales Performance: A Longitudinal Field Test," *Journal of Applied Psychology* 84 (1999): 249–59.

28. John Norcross and D. J. Vangarelli, "The Resolution Solution: Longitudinal Examination of New Year's Change Attempts," *Journal of Substance Abuse* 1 (1989): 127–34. See also John Norcross et al., "Auld Lang Syne: Success Predictors, Change Processes, and Self-Reported Outcomes of New Year's Resolvers and Nonresolvers," *Journal of Clinical Psychology* 58 (2002): 397–405.

29.   George R. Franke and Jeong-Eun Park, "Salesperson Adaptive
        Selling Behavior and Customer Orientation: A Meta-Analysis,"
        Journal of Marketing Research 43 (2006): 693–702. See also
        Rosann Spiro and Barton Weitz, "Adaptive Selling:
        Conceptualization, Measurement and Nomological Validity,"
        Journal of Marketing Research 27 (1990): 61–69.

30.   Stephen Kraus, *Psychological Foundations of Success: A Harvard-
        Trained Scientist Separates the Science of Success from Self-Help
        Snake Oil* (San Francisco: ChangePlanet Press, 2002), pp. 82–83.

31.   Ibid., pp. 42–44.

Chapter Three:
The Passion of the Prospect

1.   Freud is often quoted as saying love and work are the essence
        of mental health and the objectives of psychotherapy.
        According to the Freud museum, this was psychoanalyst Erik
        Erikson's characterization of Freud's thinking, rather than
        Freud's explicit point of view; see http://www.freud.org.uk
        /about/faq.

2.   For an archive of "right track/wrong track" and similar polling
        questions from a variety of firms, see http://www.pollingre-
        port.com/right.htm; accessed September 10, 2010.

3.   Phil Wahba and Jessica Wohl, "Retail Holiday Sales
        Improve After Dismal 2008," Reuters, December 28, 2009;
        http://www.reuters.com/article/idUSTRE5BR0HP20091228;
        accessed September 10, 2010. See also http://www.gallup.com/

poll/124283/christmas-spending-forecast-reverts-record-
2008-lows.aspx.

Chapter Four:
The Passion of the Product

1. Clive Coates, *Côte d'Or: A Celebration of the Great Wines of
   Burgundy* (Berkeley, Calif.: University of California Press,
   1997), p. 596.

2. Bruce Palling, "The Best Wine in the World," *More Intelligent
   Life*; http://moreintelligentlife.com/story/best-wine-world;
   accessed September 10, 2010.

3. Quoted in "Modern Living: Channel No. 1." *Time*, Monday,
   Jan. 25, 1971. Available at http://www.time.com/time/
   magazine/article/0,9171,904672-3,00.html; accessed October
   17, 2010.

4. For example, in Denver, prices rose in "neighborhoods that
   are very valuable—old historic neighborhoods. Their values
   have historically held up just because there is a limited
   supply. They are located very centrally, and they are in fairly
   affluent areas," says Ryan Tomazin, Integrated Asset Services,
   a company that tracks real estate prices (cited in Mike Mullen,
   "Some Home Prices Are Actually Rising in Denver,"
   http://money.usnews.com/money/personal-finance/real-
   estate/articles/2008/04/04/some-home-prices-are-actually-
   rising-in-denver.html; posted April 4, 2008; accessed
   September 10, 2010).

5. David Brough, "Record Diamond Prices Spark Fears Over Speculation," Reuters; http://www.reuters.com/article/idUSL126151820080312; posted March 12, 2008; accessed September 10, 2010.

Chapter Six:
From Passion to Execution

1. For information about the National Weight Control Registry and the research based on it, visit http://www.nwcr.ws.

2. Richard Wiseman, "The Luck Factor," *Skeptical Inquirer*, May/June 2003; http://www.richardwiseman.com/resources/The_Luck_Factor.pdf; accessed September 10, 2010.

3. Lawrence Tabak, "If Your Goal Is Success, Don't Consult These Gurus," *Fast Company*, December 31, 1996; http://www.fastcompany.com/magazine/06/cdu.html; accessed September 10, 2010.

4. For a detailed review of the goal-setting literature, and documentation of the findings summarized here, see Stephen Kraus, *Psychological Foundations of Success: A Harvard-Trained Scientist Separates the Science of Success from Self-Help Snake Oil* (San Francisco: ChangePlanet Press, 2002).

5. Sonja Lyubomirsky, Laura King, and Ed Diener, "The Benefits of Frequent Positive Affect: Does Happiness Lead to Success?" *Psychological Bulletin* 131 (November 2005): 803–55.

Index

About the Authors

Jim Taylor, Vice Chairman of Harrison Group, is among the country's most respected marketing and branding consultants and has sold billons of dollars in professional services during his career. At Harrison Group, Jim directs syndicated research, consulting projects, and services to customers in the luxury, real estate, and financial services categories. Jim's current clients include American Express and American Express Publishing, Chanel, Gucci, Bombardier/Flexjet, Montage Hotels, Dividend Capital Corp., UBS Private Wealth Management, Keeneland Farms, Fairmont Hotels, and Neiman Marcus, with active engagements covering targeting, brand strategy, market structure, sales forecasting, and concept development and ratification.

Jim has served as Chief Executive Officer of Yankelovich, Skelly & White; later, he was Executive Vice President and head of Hill & Knowlton's flagship New York office. He was Chief Marketing Officer and partner at Ernst & Young, and he held similar positions at Gateway Computers, Iomega Corporation, and Lyle Anderson Company. Named "Marketer of the Year" by *BrandWeek*, one of America's five leading business futurists by the *Wall Street Journal*, and among its distinguished alumni by his alma mater, Michigan State, Jim is a highly sought-after speaker on matters of technology; marketplace strategy; wealth marketing; trends in U.S. and international business; brand persona; and the integration of technology, culture, and business profitability. He has lectured at many of the country's leading universities, including Harvard and Stanford, and for major business, governmental, and civic organizations. He has contributed articles to national publications such as *Advertising Age*, *American Demographics*, the *New York Times*, the *Wall Street Journal*, the *Financial Times*, and *USA Today*.

Jim directs the *Survey of Affluence and Wealth in America* mentioned in this book, as well as syndicated studies on women, teens, and general-population issues. Jim is co-author of *The New Elite: Inside the Minds of the Truly Wealthy*; his other books include *The 500 Year Delta: What Happens After What Comes Next* and *The Visionary's Handbook: Nine Paradoxes That Will Shape the Future of Your Business*. Jim received his Ph.D. in communications from Michigan State.

* * *

Stephen Kraus is a recognized expert in consumer behavior, social trends, and sales training. With over two decades of experience in market research and social science, he provides consulting and research services to some of the world's most successful companies. Coauthor of *The New Elite: Inside the Minds of the Truly Wealthy*, Steve is also author of *Psychological Foundations of Success: A Harvard-Trained Scientist Separates the Science of Success from Self-Help Snake Oil*. His articles have appeared in *BrandWeek*, *AdWeek*, the *San Francisco Chronicle*, *Contemporary Psychology*, and a variety of scientific journals.

Steve is a featured speaker at conferences across the country, where he discusses his insights into human behavior and their marketing implications for fields as diverse as technology, financial services, retail sales, media, and packaged goods. He has also spoken at numerous scientific conferences, including those held by the American Psychological Association and the Society of Consumer Psychology.

Steve was previously Vice President of Harrison Group and President of Next Level Sciences, and he spent six years as a Partner with Yankelovich Partners, where he directed the Yankelovich Monitor—the longest continuously running study of consumer attitudes and lifestyles in America. Steve received his Ph.D. in social psychology from Harvard University, and he twice won Harvard's award for excellence in teaching.

* * *

Doug Harrison is the founding member of Harrison Group, which he established in 1996, building it from a single-person operation to one of the leading strategic research companies in the world. Harrison Group specializes in marrying attitudinal and behavioral information in producing actionable market segmentations, positioning/brand equity evaluations, new product forecasts, and product/price/design optimization—all with the goal of understanding the volume impact of marketing actions.

Prior to Harrison Group, Doug ran strategic research and volumetric forecasting at Yankelovich Partners. A veteran of over 700 forecasting studies, he has directed the brand positioning, product development, and targeting strategies for some of the world's largest companies and brands, including Coca-Cola, Microsoft, Motorola, American Express, McDonald's, Home Depot, Sara Lee, Honda, Yamaha, Louis Vuitton, T-Mobile, Neiman Marcus, Four Seasons, GlaxoSmithKline, Fleet Bank, Scotts LawnService, and InBev. Coauthor of *The New Elite: Inside the Mind of America's Truly Wealthy*, Doug has a BS in business and marketing from Cornell University.

* * *

ABOUT HARRISON GROUP

Harrison Group is a market research and strategy firm head-quartered in Waterbury, Connecticut, with offices in Boston, Seattle, and Phoenix. Harrison Group specializes in concept testing, forecasting, segmentation, branding, business consulting, and market modeling for some of America's top corporations, including financial services firms; software, technology, and packaged goods companies; retailers; pharmaceutical manufacturers; and interactive entertainment companies. Harrison Group has research and consulting practices devoted to, among other specialties, wealthy consumers, luxury markets, and sales training. In August 2010, Harrison Group agreed to be acquired by YouGov plc, a publicly traded firm recognized as a global market leader in survey and market research, political polling, panel management, research operations, and business consulting.

We pride ourselves on providing clients definitive guidance on business decisions. We like to believe our firm is characterized by a passion for the truth—our hallmark is an intense curiosity about the truth of human ambition, acquisitiveness, engagement, market behavior, and social distinction.